JOURNEY OF 1,000 BREATHS

WISDOM YOU BROUGHT TO SOLEIL'S SALT CAVE

DARYL BROWNE

CHAPTER 1

Treasure those who find ways to despise;
Their misdirected abilities to recognize
Are the ones we use to regress or to rise.

Thoughts and work are a small part.
The biggest piece of all is your heart.
With it, whatever you do will be art.

You will overcome the insurmountable
By holding only yourself accountable;
Draw upon what feels most true.[1]

A day of kindness costs so little
So even if you're feeling brittle,
Do something to share a giggle.

Fear was being sold and they bought it,
Blame was being thrown and you caught it;
Do not pass it back, just gently drop it.

What if you have nothing left to earn -
No new next offers over which to churn?
You're richest when you forget to yearn.

If an "I love you" feels transactional,
Stop. Give an "I love you" intentional,
Letting your "I love" be unconditional.

The point of the story is not to lay laws,
But to give you some time to just pause
And maybe rewrite your own "because."

What's really going on eludes you
Until you decide to know the truth
By deciding to see right through.

If you need to yell to be heard,
When it's calm, you'll sound absurd:
Go where they hear your words.

Sometimes in order to avoid feeling shame,
The mind looks anywhere else to find blame
Rather than at the very one who complains.

Compared to them, your rise has been quick,
But it doesn't mean you're doing what fits.
Start getting better, not just better at this.

To kind to yourself through compliments
Ones that sound sincere and heaven-sent
And are unrelated to any accomplishment.

Would you prefer to be right or get results,
Or be the one with whom everyone consults
Or to be blessed with the steadiest pulse?

You are obliged to use your critical mind
To think your own way through this time.
You must do more than hope it goes fine.

Get back in the habit, without excuse.
Whatever's in the way, do cut it loose.
Whatever's been learned, put it to use.

There are 1,000 paths to 1,000 places so
Welcome the one in front of your face as
A road to be enjoyed at a personal pace.

Being understood will never be required.
Just keep finding new ways to be inspired,
Looking only and ever and inward higher.

Patience, because you're still building
Making real by virtue of sheer willing
So today let nothingness be fulfilling.

Welcome the tears. They are a good sign:
You are tender and vulnerable by design.
Love - you need no one else to be kind.

As keeper of this space, it is your role
To maintain a voice that is your own
And over key details, practice control.

Things work out, you already know that.
It doesn't mean you should just sit back.
But it does mean you can certainly relax.

Parts of the journey will feel exciting,
Others will seem a little frightening;
What will help is to do some writing.

Whether you find wrong turns unamusing,
Or laugh all throughout winning or losing,
Either way, keep doing what you're doing.

Being free means you are able to be open.
So allow love to bubble into this notion,
That you've only seen a bit of your ocean.

As you align, the ideas will overflow,
Blending with what you've already grown
To make something that is all your own.

Who do you know who's wiser than you?
Are they a part of your social group?
If not, find a way to make this true.

Neither fact nor opinion lives eternally
So why should you feel anything but ease?
Take a breath and enjoy the witnessing.

It will not matter in the long run.
What will matter is that you had fun.
Can you do this before you get done?

Forget about what could come next,
Just keep letting air into your chest
And back out again. Forget the rest.

Use your mind to point to every option,
But let your heart pick, no precaution;
This is the journey - not some auction.

It is more important to keep things fresh
Than it is to think about your own success
As long as you feel some sense of progress.

If you love what you do, share it freely
Because once you manifest your dreaming
Wealth has already started streaming.

You are not here to cling or to clutch.
You are not to archive details and such.
Today, you are to be exactly this much.

Though that gave a good reason to fuss,
Grow numb to such cyclical stimulus -
Endure it to do exactly what you must.

Don't think of it as some big decision.
No, think of it as a gradual transition
Toward you, and away from tradition.

You are gathering allies as you go along
And sometimes the mix will feel wrong.
Difficult partnerships make you strong.

Beyond stopping by to greet it,
Caring means you have to feed it
As often as nourishment is needed.

Time will change you - body, mind and soul.
But what keeps you from growing wearily old
Is your ability to remain flexible and bold.

If you'll dare to use the simplest tools,
You'll help free others from rigid rules
And have a method you can always use.

Be reminded by talking with someone older
Of when your own winters were much colder.
Let memory serve to make you even bolder.

Dedication merely clears the way:
Structure is what ensures you stay
Right in the heart of the interplay.

Yes, no matter which direction you choose,
Change is coming, no matter what you do.
So no matter what, figure out what is true.

You are not to blame - you are responsible -
And this makes you so much more powerful
As you realize something truly meaningful.

Overcoming negativity is a noble pursuit,
But you can do far more. That's the truth.
Courageously imagine. Lovingly produce.

Better decisions ask for better questions
About matters not normally mentioned;
Honesty will help set the best intention.

To feel obligated is to ignore yourself,
Lose your time and squander all wealth.
Choose all you do: this creates health.

Whether or not you see them as signs,
They're appearing to you all the time,
Not so much to teach - but to remind.

This is just what becoming looks like -
No longer back there, nor fully in sight
Peeling back layer upon layer of mights.

Consider as much as possible beforehand,
But when it's time, simply do all you can,
Not what you don't quite yet understand.

On being full we put too much emphasis.
What can be added to what is plenteous?
For there is no room without emptiness.

Your thoughts are getting very complex -
You're getting your own lightness vexed:
Your heart wants what's simple and fresh.

The reason to be mindful of comfort?
You may forget what you've come for.
The uncomfortable become triumphant.

Don't theorize - try out each one fully.
Don't let either of them become a bully.
Above all, do not commit prematurely.

No one else can direct you exactly what
From your daily rituals you need to cut
So decide for yourself which digs a rut.

Slow down - it is your earnestness
That brings out all your very best,
And draws wisdom out of patience.

Some conversations wander in the dark,
Others become an inspirational spark.
Give the next conversation your heart.

This time, you should keep quiet,
So saboteurs cannot come find it:
Be as busy as ever, but also silent.

There are 100 ways to go where you wish
This would be obvious if you were a fish,
No paths - a whole sea in which to swish.

There will always be new places to go,
To taste or to touch or to see or know.
Life is long, so make your process slow.

Knowing what you have is no small feat,
Like tasting ingredients in all you eat
So take your time by taking a seat.

If you see that you've come back here again,
And as for returning, don't remember when,
Breathe in fresh knowing, to a count of ten.

A sense of purpose will keep you healthy
And if it does not also make you wealthy
The reward's just nearby being stealthy.

Interruptions - they tell you a lot
About what you didn't wish to stop
And what you instinctively dropped.

Pay attention to what ebbs and flows and
Look past to what neither comes nor goes
This is the You without highs or lows.

Trust the closest examples of success
Rather than going away to be blessed;
Make results easier for time to test.

Wherever silence hides a fear
The greatest healer is the ear
That listens until all is clear.

It is time for a change in your conversation -
To listen much longer, make fewer declarations
And speak about insights, not just frustrations.

If it comes apart after awhile
Or can go in and out of style,
Toss it out and onto the pile.

You don't have to work - you have to align
In order to achieve anything one-of-a-kind:
Don't strain your back - ease your mind.

Certain memories that still feel like loss
Are not at all about you paying life's cost,
They feel like this to keep your heart soft.

In order to help, they must first know
That you need help to continue to go.
They only see this by what you show.

Make yourself a double promise:
That you will get through this
And your moves will be swift.

Since there are so many forces at play,
You do best to let go, come what may:
See how everything happens anyway.

Know what your energy flows from and to.
Also mind what your energy flows through,
Because that affects your effectiveness too.

Take that road - what is there to lose?
If anything, it will help you to choose
Since it is better to try than to refuse.

You could accomplish this all by yourself
But it is time to learn to be open to help
That can make this go better than well.

Look at it with your own eyes. Go. See.
Because the picture is still incomplete
And you must have it before you agree.

Can you see yourself as a conduit?
Realize you're not here to "do it."
Let yourself just sit here and intuit.

Your ego is too concerned with results.
That is why it pressures you to consult,
Trying to save itself from the catapult.

Your tone tends to turn its harshest
Where your inner night is darkest;
Let your dawn light up this forest.

What are they selling - and to whom?
Find this out or your time is doomed
To whatever they schedule, and soon.

Those addicted to information
Lose themselves in observation.
Find yourself lost in creation.

Since you're open to better possibilities
Others will come bearing more of these;
Choose the option that comes with keys.

Know good from bad kinds of stress.
Give in to mayhem or give in to rest.
Lay down weary and rise up the best.

Be unpredictable. Keep your responses fluid
So that whatever's up ahead, you adjust to it
And rather than obey a plan, naturally intuit.

The level of choices you have to make
Keep rising with each risk you take,
So be aware of how much is at stake.

Do you pour your time into your will?
Or do you leave some for chance to fill?
Is there enough room to avoid a spill?

You don't have to like what they bring.
Nor act as if you consider it interesting.
Get better at enjoying your own thing.

It may not be time for the actual words,
But you can start simply living it at first
So the blossoming can go on undisturbed.

As you come to the close of a chapter,
See if you caught what you were after
And unburied a treasure of laughter.

Where in your character does that fit?
Might it help or hurt the rest of this?
Can you create a life lived without it?

Appreciating is now your most useful skill:
It makes what seemed empty somehow fill,
And what you couldn't do, what you will.

You were speaking before you were fluent
And building before needing a blueprint;
Continue to trust in your own movement.

If you keep on coming back as you like,
It will keep bringing you back to 'might.'
No. Head to the farthest thing in sight.

There's how they describe it,
And there's how it really is:
From which do you benefit?

Let someone else be busy talking about it -
Because narrators eventually tire and quit.
Be the one who works at the center of this.

Today brings another treasure trove more
Of uncanny, precious coincidences galore
Delivered right to your schedule's door.

When you feel yourself drifting inside,
Momentum is all that will save your mind
And your deadlines from falling behind.

Make action certain. Make action swift.
Make the kind of decision that is quick.
Nimble non-attachment has its benefits.

CHAPTER 2

Your intensity will never be a match
For what easeful alignment can catch
Nor for an itch only time can scratch.

Life is already getting better.
You've outlasted the weather.
Everything has come together.

Too many work hard; too few work smart.
Savvy ends where the strong back starts so
Conserve your power and use other parts.

Give up social norms for personal depth.
Deviate from all those regimented steps.
Your destiny is an unpaved path ahead.

Not knowing how things will play out,
Sharpen the focus on what you're about
And then more good things will sprout.

On a scale you never dreamed to imagine,
In a way you could not begin to fathom,
The most incredible things just happen.

With everything, there are other levels,
So let the approach you take be gentle.
To ensure your options remain several.

You were invited to this grand exposition
Not given a ticket for general admission,
But sought out to be the perfect addition.

And so what is a lifetime of experience worth
If a deep sense of purpose doesn't come first?
A refreshing drink is useless without thirst.

It's easy to get caught up in the day
And the circus of what people may say
But just keep making your own way.

Not an issue about which to think twice:
Own your space. This is serious advice -
You're creating your version of paradise.

A big part of momentum is removal
Of influences that can never be useful
As you discover your spirit's approval.

You will never get enough -
You will only have enough -
Once you decide, "Enough."

If you're hearing from just one source
You're ignoring life's far greater force
Available all along your entire course.

You are not the mindset you identify with,
Nor are you the habits to which you stick -
You are this essence that makes each shift.

You're given a gift; do you go and sell it?
Do you move to take ownership or credit?
Just how should you share what is given?

You can work at something for so long
That it can cease to make you strong.
There is somewhere else you belong.

In matters of eating, fitness and wealth
Find one way each day to push yourself:
Do what you learned despite what's felt.

Let them build trust with you slowly.
This moment isn't your one nor only -
Take your time and proceed - slowly...

Sharing ideas is a partnership practice
That both opens up and lightens baggage.
Such an alliance can brave any passage.

After a while, you won't be able to stop
Your very own rhythm won't let you drop;
By keeping tempo, you'll reach the top.

If conversations take a superficial turn
Don't let your impatience ignite or burn
The listening lesson you need to learn.

A little more organization will help
So you can daily enhance your health,
Which is the essence of useful wealth.

Slow down, stop moving so fervently.
That is not leading toward harmony,
Which is now all that is necessary.

Be as interested in giving as in getting
Because it is as important to be letting
Others enjoy the pleasure of begetting.

Don't say you can't - say that you don't.
Though you surely can, you simply won't.
Practice this until it is fully your own.

Frustration weeds up the empty space
Wherever commitment isn't yet laid;
Hands in dirt is how a garden's made.

Determine its genuine value.
Get good at it. You have to:
Soon others will ask you.

You need certainty, now more than ever.
Because certainty makes its own weather
And will keep all your energies together.

Making a new one may break two old,
But take it lightly if someone scolds.
Keep causing more things to unfold.

Before the dawn it will get dark,
So use the light within your heart
If you need to make an early start.

When someone resonates deeply to you,
Pause to find out what else they value
And this may uncover more inner truth.

You get to write this story of life
So draft and craft until it is right
Better than your dreams at night.

The energy you put in can be rough or easy:
The first kind is stormy - the other, breezy.
Would you rather travel fiercely or freely?

The shortcut never works out that way,
Though it does remind how not to behave
When next you choose to stick or stray.

Open up, lean back, look up and extend.
Stretch out past every limit's very end,
And past whoever wants to know when.

If there are conditions, love is held ransom,
Which can offer less in the way of expansion,
Which is not something to take a chance on.

By neither apathy nor habit be overtaken
Because whenever one of them's forsaken,
It blames the other for troublemaking.

The day is meant for little investments,
Small, key decisions, subtle sentiments.
Where you are going's a half step ahead.

Feel and then think; think and then do,
In this order and you'll follow through.
To bloom, you need an emotional root.

It was generous of you to go over there -
But of overextending yourself, do beware:
You are long overdue for extensive self-care.

Delay for as long as your ego requires.
Existence can wait a much longer while,
Or you and Habit could just reconcile.

Whenever you feel things go off-course,
Think your way right back to the source:
Make sure there is more flow than force.

Before you rush to fix their problems,
Make sure they're real enough to solve
Before getting yourself fully involved.

You are the only one in your way:
Simply hear some of what you say.
Change your language this very day.

Finish the ones now growing old
And start adding some newer goals
So the rest of you can yet unfold.

It will hurt so much you won't want to go on.
But the journey's the only place you belong,
And the journey is what will make you strong.

If you get tired, take that as your sign
That part of you is getting left behind.
It should be a deepening - not a grind.

Those you're happiest to see again return
Not for any extra love they hope to earn,
But because you don't just glow, you burn.

By itself it should not have hurt.
Maybe it did because of past work.
Either way, treat it as a landmark.

What does love mean to you now?
Has it changed - and if so how?
What else will your life endow?

It's been brewing for quite some time
And now you can't pout, deny, or whine;
You can only stop, accept and realign.

Of course you know how to protect,
But open up the gates and connect
With all the villagers you affect.

There are so many powerful words to use,
Your holiest act is to mercifully choose
Which to deliver and which ones to lose.

One year cannot hold extra months.
One guard cannot protect two fronts.
You should do much less, at once.

If even now they are still looking back,
Reminiscing, narrating, rehashing past,
Are you in fact with those who will act?

Making yourself out as hero or villain
Is limiting - even if it feels fulfilling,
A role too flat for anyone to be filling.

Hopefully you have not forgotten this:
You can learn more from your opposite
Than you can from what just won't fit.

Make certain necessary sacrifices
To steer things away from a crisis
It will be hard, but be decisive.

Take heart - it is coming soon,
Bigger than any monetary boon.
All you have to do is make room.

What you're making will last a long time.
Others will use it along their own climb.
Find their future thanks in subtle signs.

Make the space to be loved and be lover.
This becomes impossible amongst clutter,
So, out with what takes you no further.

It is uncooked opinion that alienates
By exclaiming before it contemplates,
Letting true conversation go to waste.

Before life can be what you make it
Life's ears need to hear you say it -
That you've now chosen to commit.

Is there a schedule you need to keep?
Can you stop and enjoy what you see?
Is it alright to arrive eventually?

The quality of what comes in is essential
Because of how it grows your potential and
How it can make that growth exponential.

You've done so much - stop and remember.
You grew this blaze from just an ember
And given love that will last forever.

You are most you when you are a channel,
And things greater than you could handle
Get done simply by lighting your candle.

A slump is not to be avoided -
But how your cycle is pointed
So nothingness can be enjoyed.

Rise - it is now the time for you to rise,
To face the master you already are inside,
And see yourself from behind your eyes.

Do any of them seem happier than you
Living the way you dream to live too?
Examine every detail, not just a few.

You've decided. Let that be that.
To decide without turning back
Generates the power to attract.

Can you see how you've repeated enough?
Do you see there's no more to gain from
Continuing with no point to speak of?

Were you supposed to live, frozen there
As if their fears should get you scared?
It is alright to say you just don't care.

Half of the journey is realizing you're there,
Deep in the place you'd been told to beware.
The rest is navigating your route elsewhere.

To get to the heart of this matter,
Listen to some of the daily chatter
And filter out the nonsense faster.

Why does it have to be wrapped so tight?
Does this symbolize a desire to be right?
Loosen: discover both meanings of light.

Rejection can make you feel vulnerable,
But you're wrong - it's nothing personal:
You're about to become more versatile.

Are you there more than you realize?
Ask someone with a fresh set of eyes -
As denial can put on a clever disguise.

About what comes first, next and last,
That stale advice belongs in the trash;
Live life in to out - not front to back.

Whenever you get stuck in the middle,
It's harder to saw, easier to whittle.
It's easier to do it little by little.

In choosing which way to go forth,
Which hallways lead to which doors?
And which lead to how many more?

Where there is space, things rush to fill,
And do so again and again, right up until
It's cleared with intention backed by will.

Turn right around and knock once more.
But this time knock harder on that door,
And when it opens, go on in self-assured.

The habit of taking a small step today
Is what gets obstacles out of your way
And keeps those who waste time at bay.

Be sad for as long as you must and move on.
You don't need to be ready, or even strong.
Just find a nearby path you can walk along.

Once you start genuinely expressing,
What feels like a public undressing,
Is stripping away second-guessing.

If you feel uncertain where to go again
Or cannot begin to decide exactly when,
Breathe this mind out to a count of ten.

You need to keep heading this same way
For what you'll get to hear yourself say
As you find better ways to do each day.

Hold this ground. Do not advance.
Plant both feet. Own this stance,
Unmoved - as if deep in a trance.

Fitness can serve as your best medicine
To keep any negativity from getting in
And keep you focused on how you'll win.

In being the lone expert, there is no use,
For talent and skill are just a thin excuse
For why they just want to be around you.

Because time is the only asset you get,
Part from everyone you find wasting it
And study anyone who's schedule is set.

You have chopped down that rotted tree -
The leaning decay of all limiting beliefs,
So newer growth can branch out freely.

If you catch yourself correcting another
Stop yourself from speaking any further
Until you can appreciate what you heard.

Make your own decision,
Uphold your own vision
And by each be driven.

Check they know what they're talking about,
That they understand their work in and out,
And begin with mind, then end with mouth.

Some things will never be worth doing,
Since they're not what you're pursuing;
Pour the time into what you're brewing.

Knowing where to draw your line
Is going to take a bit more time.
Exactly where, is for you to find.

Onto your approach, does it makes sense?
Which part of it is feeling odd or dense?
How could you feel light yet immense?

CHAPTER 3

The notion that you haven't done it right
Is fine once you see each mistake as light
That shows you a bit more in your night.

Exciting times are nearly upon you,
Not because of anything you'll do,
But because of what comes through.

So much can be said in one single glance
That one moment holds enough chances
To behold all the deeper circumstances.

You did things that were ingredients for now
With no way back then to have any idea how:
Tomorrow already knows today turns around.

Check on their work before they return.
Pay those who sell, just what they earn.
In business, charity is not the concern.

What's most important, tackle first.
Realize if it were hunger or thirst,
Not doing so would soon be worse.

Problems are a sign of growth.
Mastery is growth grown old.
Take the journey of unknowns.

Whatever you want, match in attitude
And it will come to you rather soon.
You have already lived your proof.

First there's what you should be doing,
Then there's what you're quietly brewing;
All else you're just naturally excluding.

Everyone hurts, so show them you care
And they will come in from everywhere
To support you - not just stop and stare.

Your evolution can happen overnight,
Or it can be a long, drawn-out fight;
Either way, it is going to be alright.

Can you move through today without a plan?
It's an easier way to watch butterflies land
And wiggle your toes in thoughts like sand.

For some, complaining is a form of fitness.
But only listen long enough to bear witness
To what's louder and softer - forgiveness.

Knowing just what you want is marvelous,
But if it turns you more and more serious,
Start over with what can keep you curious.

So much of it lives within the delivery
That you will excel as soon as you see
What you can give instead of receive.

Don't have to live fearing the worst,
But why not put certain things first?
Peace of mind takes such little work.

Turning back to find the way is silly.
It is not warm back there, it's chilly.
Turn to the sun as if you were a lily.

Part of your work must be public
So people can hold it and touch it
And share their love because of it.

How deep inside your precious home
Do you let someone you don't know?
It probably means you should say no.

Ranking yourself from expert to novice
Only adds sand to a desert of nonsense;
Put your focus on remaining conscious.

Dismantling doubt takes much more time
Than moving forward in one straight line
Be original later - for now, just rhyme.

There's a time for hearing, but not now;
This is the time to tilt your head down
And work in isolation, no matter how.

You can look at this in a much better way
So there will be even better things to say
Which will benefit you as soon as today.

What they do may even deeply annoy,
But irritation is the mind's best ploy.
Work on yourself; see past this decoy.

You're going to end up feeling stress.
But the point is what you'll feel next:
Pain or purpose when you do it again.

Trust your ears even more than your eyes
And you will soon be pleasantly surprised
At how easy it is to know things' insides.

You didn't wish to be where you are now,
But what you've created deserves a bow -
Because you fell in but flew yourself out.

If you wish it would all go more quickly
Your mind is heading somewhere prickly;
To your heart's time just keep sticking.

As you're now finishing,
Here's to new beginnings!
By starting you are winning.

By seeing opportunity in bad weather,
You bring the farthest parts together
And create something beyond measure.

Whatever seems out of control and absurd,
Looks so whenever your vision is blurred.
Clarity appears as you choose your words.

You can't reverse anyone's misperception,
Or undo doubt with any excuse you mention:
All you can do is live your own intention.

When you flinch at the price,
You're looking in from outside:
The amount is a measure of time.

What you are working toward will arrive
Along with a feeling one cannot describe
As anything except proof of what's inside.

You have to trust that greatness builds,
Never outward from more and more frills,
But ever-inward from daily-honed skills.

Asking to find out why
Is one of the clear signs:
Trust your own insight.

You absolutely have to speak up for yourself,
For your time, but most of all, your health;
Only you can know you down to your cells.

You are going to have make a sacrifice
That some will say is paying the price:
It is the decision to live your own life.

To finally decide on what you should do,
Rather than start to look anywhere new,
Think your way up to the clearest view.

Giving it your voice is a very serious step:
You own the essence of what you say next,
So let your words be fruitful yet content.

It's time to journey upstream -
To the source of your mystery
To your answer's beginning.

Talking and talking and talking it through
Will likely start to shake something loose
That has attached itself but serves no use.

Listen closest to what is sitting silent.
Clues that were never openly expressed
Point directly into what's truly meant.

You'll have more to offer if you come back
After time away, because distance attracts
Things well beyond this one single track.

It may take all you have to get back up.
Know this is not a should - it is a must:
Rise again with renewed love and trust.

Put yourself in the right place as well.
This lessens the need for you to sell
And allows your story itself to tell.

It may take a shock to make you believe
But the facts were not given to deceive;
There are habits you must forever leave.

You've done a lot quickly. Now slow down
To truly meet people and just look around
And feel all the power of common ground.

When your roots feel stretched thin,
Maybe it's because the patch you're in
Will be the forest your tree begins.

Filling up on stories may feel enough -
But what's actually filling you is a love
That words are just traveling on top of.

Between knowing everything or everyone,
The first will get more and more done,
The last will grow more and more love.

Of the things you should be talking about
Negative small talk should never come out
Let praises and plans control your mouth.

This something you're yearning to do -
Don't finish it as something to prove -
Let it be something that enjoys You too.

Learn most from whoever complains
About how their life has remained,
And see what you two do the same.

Today is your invitation to shed layers,
To be rid of charlatans and soothsayers,
To start over with a new set of prayers.

The way ahead's job is not to be clear -
The way ahead's job is to show you fear
Was a way that is neither now nor here.

Out of love you have invited this delay
But soon enough, you must get underway
So prepare for what you'll have to say.

Regardless of your feeling ready,
Shed, shed and keep on shedding.
Let the peeling away be unending.

Rather than constantly feeling surprised,
What would it be like to feel energized?
Could this question become your guide?

Though talking can get so intriguing,
You are here for more than a meeting:
Find out what you can be completing.

If there is a parade behind you, let it play.
So long as it does not start to lead the way.
Behind, never ahead, is the place for praise.

When they say it is too complicated,
Listen with a great deal of patience.
You did the work - they just waited.

Think of it as if you're building a chain,
Either the kind that holds and maintains,
Or the kind that pulls incredible weight.

If you've run before, you may run again,
Until it is time for your running to end,
Which only you decide where and when.

Wanting them to come to you is futile.
First you need to make yourself useful
By finding out what to them is crucial.

Focusing on the good ones or the bad
Is a socially-accepted way to go mad;
Live for moments you have, not had.

Certain mistakes can cost you much more
Than anything you could have planned for
So prevent them with organization galore.

Whether visibly or just inwardly churning,
Is someting in you sitting there squirming?
Consciously forgetting is your new learning.

Before you vouch, make sure they qualify.
Listen to accomplishments, not to alibis.
Choose making sure over answering why.

This time you know just where to search -
Exactly where you thought to look first.
Trust your instinct as if it were thirst.

Beware unending trips to life's shops.
No one will tell you it's time to stop.
Decide what to buy and what to not.

What you are doing is considered pursuit
Of what you have greatest attachment to.
Without your chasing, would it find you?

Of course you're not always right,
But you've got incredible insight
To move from darkness into light.

One of the best ways to offer help
Is to take amazing care of yourself
To show what goes into being well.

Instead of wondering about the other side
And gathering knowledge that feeds pride,
Why not appreciate your own lovely stride?

You don't need to think ill of anyone,
Just let the course of their habits run
And weigh for yourself the outcome.

Work on your words until you are sincere
Not just saying what they expect to hear
But expressing what is loving and clear.

The schedule you'll have to keep
Would make your past-self weep;
There will be a time for sleep.

You underestimate your need for rest,
Your need to melt in a loving caress.
Your need to feel ease in your chest.

You weren't meant to tend to everything
Since you're the only one who can bring
A life expressed with your special zing.

This isn't one to think your way through,
But one to find you being something new
- a rainbow with never-before-seen hues.

Any hesitation to do as they suggest,
Or urge to stop listening to the rest
Is your intuition saying what's best.

Think of a better way to look at this
And then improve even more upon it
Why should best-cases have a limit?

Just like a rope, your patience can fray
If twisted and pulled every which way;
Mend it by giving yourself a quiet day.

You've worked on your own long enough.
It's a testament to you you didn't give up.
Now it's time to come and meet everyone.

Whatever you focus on multiplies,
And whatever you ignore subsides,
So decide what to show your eyes.

No matter the damage, keep rebuilding.
Perhaps more windows, higher ceilings?
This is flourishing, not just healing.

Do you want them to ignore their thirst?
To them, whose discomfort feels worst?
Have you helped them ease theirs first?

With more than enough on your plate,
You know it's time for you to delegate.
So find someone who can demonstrate.

As good as it is to know your dislikes,
Which activities fill you with delight?
Choosing these will shine your light.

Masters of details are junk collectors.
Pupils of perspective are the investors,
The ones to search out as your mentors.

A community has chosen to encircle
What you set up and it's wonderful,
Because this support is so durable.

It's alright to let your schedule bend,
But you must return to what you intend
To see your original goals to the end.

Get things ready for what's on the way.
What needs to go and what should stay?
Make haste as if you had only this day!

Pull yourself away from too much study;
Memorizing turns a mind's waters muddy.
More information is what you don't need.

As unpleasant a thought as it may be,
Things are only ever called upsetting
If unflattering angles are reflecting.

The conversation hasn't happened just yet,
Even though everything else has been set -
So go in seeing your needs as already met.

What is worthwhile takes effort -
Not reading a book by each letter,
But dedicating to growing better.

Do not be drastic - that is ineffective;
You should try to be more introspective
So that your gains are all protected.

Deal with it before it gets any bigger;
So far there is nothing it can trigger
Since you outdo it in will and vigor.

CHAPTER 4

What any experience will mean
All depends on your philosophy
So why not use one that's lean?

Take the time to pick what matters most
By looking at the things you keep close
And revising your list of who you host.

Your openness is what gives them permission
To tell of ideas that go far past idle wishing,
Finding their way just by having you listen.

Hold those fears in two closed hands
And let them escape as grains of sand
Each too small to make any demands.

Do you find yourself overtasked again?
Do you wonder when this cycle will end?
Are you willing to love yet not bend?

So it's not over before it ever begins,
Forget about whether it loses or wins:
Can you make it feel lighter than this?

Thought-circles will dizzy your peace
For years until you tell them to cease
So you can distinguish west from east.

If you knew the future, would it matter?
Today looks through a window of chatter
That tomorrow plans to open or shatter.

Their imaginations don't need words to see
What you want to share and genuinely feel.
They need what is faced, lived, and real.

Leaving your comfort zone just to do so
May be self-sabotaging today's momentum.
Your instinct already knows how to go.

Figure out a way for it to remain fun
Because you'll recall when it is done
How fully-enjoyed, not how well-run.

What is the essence of what you talk about?
Because you grow whatever you speak aloud,
So decide what kind of talk will be allowed.

Certain causes produce certain effects
So you already know what happens next
Just looking at what to what connects.

At this point, it may just be a whisper,
Because your body trusts you will listen
Without needing it shouted or written.

If what you're told contradicts
Something you just feel within,
You're not what needs to be fixed.

Once you give away what matters most
You become the universe's gracious host
Keeping nothing but your openness close.

It's wise to learn from those who fail,
But beware those who repeatedly flail;
Ask about the direction of their sail.

Sometimes you don't get to decide
What pushes your plan on its side;
Your job is to make things right.

Caution only makes more sense
When sitting atop an old fence.
Come down and openly express.

Wait before calling circumstance unfair.
Instead find the opportunity to be aware
Of what needs work, and precisely where.

Take a moment to see it from the finish
And see what stress this does diminish;
To be most effective, remain a witness.

When you want everything to stop
To give you more time to gear up,
Tell this feeling, "That's enough."

Key is to focus on just one front, else
Jeopardize the whole point of the hunt.
Relentlessly chase what it is you want.

Shift your focus away from an audience
To something somehow not as obvious:
It is in the doing that you are blessed.

To some, this may sound rotten:
History eventually gets forgotten,
Or at least not retold very often.

When taking advice from the unhappy,
Convert it to something you can carry,
Go do the opposite of what went badly.

Perhaps the only useful lesson you learn
When all you want is to stop the churn,
Is that your fire must continue to burn.

Can you imagine an infinite light?
One that gives you infinite sight?
Didn't you just turn it on inside?

Being busy is another form of fear -
Preferring to ride rather than steer;
Take the wheel, but stop right here.

You can regroup, retrain and rebound by
Leaving those who prefer to trend down.
Upward again might mean turning around.

You can see it on involved people's faces,
An inner glow that reflects engagement:
Make yourself useful in fulfilling places.

That you are so responsible in
Tending to what's meaningful
Is nothing short of wonderful.

Things get better - that is what they do.
As wishes can change, so habits can too.
It all starts with you, undeniably, You.

Let doubt have its chance to say
What it's sure is down this way,
Nod and come back out to play.

Whether as a member or out on your own,
See that your truth always stands alone,
And the mirror reflects one well-known.

Do you go where the welcome is warmest?
Or are you now willing to brave the forest,
Where favorite comforts may be poorest?

Press on yet give in when it fits;
Water crashes but can quietly sit.
Power uses what ways you give it.

Perhaps not what you'd preferred,
Perhaps even noticeably awkward,
Perhaps just the only way forward.

First, line everything up the right way:
Closest to what's most important stay;
Head into yourself, not into the fray.

Pay attention to your mood when you pay:
Ecstatic to be making financial headway
Or eagerly anticipating your next foray?

For a while it can all start to get tangled
Things coming in from every odd angle;
It's just to show what you can wrangle.

Even if it should last until you grow old,
This is nothing more than a temporary role
And is but the tiniest sliver of your soul.

Your passion is your power ignited,
Which is more than feeling excited,
It is being what's just been lighted.

This new information that you've found -
Is in your hands - to pick up or put down
Based on whether it serves you right now.

Feel, feel, and then feel some more.
That is how feet move across a floor,
And how you get to what you adore.

Just by showing up you open doors
That lock behind you and with force.
Should you still go in? Of course.

Just relax and lean back on experience,
Proof you needn't fret nor turn furious
As life likes you to not be too serious.

Generosity even toward your inner miser
Because by opening your arms out wider
Your inner creator becomes the decider.

Looking to what any given day can bring
Is tending to the wind and not the wing
Put your health before any daily thing.

What happened, happened for a reason:
To turn all of your doing into being,
As you unroll this feeling's meaning.

You mean more than you will know to
People who just seem to come then go:
Your impact doesn't need you to know.

This is not going to last forever -
Just until more pieces fit together
Or you start using your time better.

The time for travel will soon be over,
Not like turning from dazed to sober,
But like rising up from being covert.

If they feel more comfortable shouting,
Or blaming others or even just pouting,
Quietly escape: take an internal outing.

This is no longer that distant frontier.
You need to do more than dwell here,
So start focusing on the atmosphere.

Which creativity comes when alone?
Which creativity comes from home?
Which creativity comes on its own?

Go on, keep enriching yourself with
Daily-earned savings of inner wealth
By doing things that treasure health.

Is it too advanced for right now?
Is it an idea that dares the how?
For present reality does it allow?

Rather than sitting around maybe waiting
For those prone to resisting and debating,
You can be locking the door and creating.

Forgive yourself first. Have you truly?
Mentally, emotionally and spiritually?
Let go. You deserve to live peacefully.

Your peace will come from being flexible -
In your body, your mind and your schedule.
Gradually shed all but your own key rituals.

You're looking at it from the wrong side
Although you feel you've already tried;
Find someone who can act as your guide.

Carefully, carefully mind your loops -
Those thought patterns you slip into.
And once one starts, regroup, regroup.

Be mindful of the words you select
To keep your mind's ears in check.
Try out new ones and then reflect.

The act of creation is what gives life,
So everything else can move to the side
For you to be in this mode all the time.

If you wish to dodge a stampede,
The thunder is not what to heed;
Sense of direction is all you need.

It should be big! Why make it small?
If you can leap, why choose to crawl?
Since you're able, why not give it all?

Whenever you start to feel angry,
Something is telling you frankly
You need to revisit it blankly.

There is no lack, not in any given thing
You simply decide, then get in the ring,
Step, tuck, advance and take your swing.

You're expected to want something more,
And so what is all that wanting ever for?
Does it point to a place that feels pure?

When wants can just be, you've arrived.
Most never challenge the voices inside
That are a shallow part of being alive.

Your next conversation is like a key
To unlock the inner door that leads
Deep down into your soul's library.

Be mindful of what you tend to produce;
Does it put your goodness to good use?
Does it let even more creativity loose?

Revisit some of your less pressing goals
To see which ones are now stale or cold
And which if any can still serve a role.

Freedom and access - these are worth it.
The ability to step on in and be certain
That each option is pursuable and open.

And if it had happened in any other way
You would not have this awareness today;
Gather your regrets and throw them away.

Only consider advice that has proof
That does more than just toss clues;
Trust what you can thoroughly use.

No one else gets to use your voice.
No one else gets to make this choice.
No one else gets to have your poise.

Soon enough, you'll reach your limit,
The place that might tire you to visit,
But where you'll reconnect to spirit.

Still thinking about it as all or none?
Is there a place between boring and fun?
Is there a way to get this gently done?

Speak too soon and you may rouse a riot.
All the better if you can covertly try it;
Keep your goal warm, close and quiet.

You can learn volumes by listening closely
To the topics people don't mention, mostly,
And going deaf to what is said boastfully.

You uplift everything around you.
The effects are tangible and true.
Knowing this, what will you do?

There is so much you do not need to know
There is so little you need to love the flow
There are so very many ways you can grow.

Stop measuring how long it's been for now
You should stay focused on what, not how;
You've already made your ancestors proud.

Sleep waits at the other end of strength,
To prove you have done your best when
At day's end you crave nothing but rest.

Of course you'd be more comfortable knowing.
But what's coming won't do an early showing
Of all the new treasures it will be bestowing.

When you let it come to you
You know it is meant to do,
And not just something new.

It wasn't meant to make your anger burn,
It was meant to make you set your terms
And be simultaneously honest and firm.

If you're not pleased with your performance,
Take on habits that build up your endurance,
Which also serves as the best life insurance.

Eventually there are no leaders to model
Just one path-paving intention to follow
Keeping you, in the best of ways, hollow.

If you get stuck in the circle of thought
For far longer than you realize or ought,
Take one bold leap and out you will pop!

There's not one thing you do that's small:
You pass unlit lanterns along a night wall
And your torch brings light to them all.

No need to feel burdened by the pile;
When you can at least once in a while
Laugh and give it your silliest smile.

Appreciate ordeals that feel harder still,
When the intended goals go unfulfilled,
When all you truly are and own is Will.

You're already saying how it will be,
So how about wording it differently?
Start using new words immediately.

How will it go, if you start and then stop?
What's the point if you catch and then drop?
You need to tend to this as a lifelong crop.

This is but one way to see things. Tilt
To notice how your perspective's filled
With details that only matter until…

There's how you're choosing to see it unfold,
Then there's how others want this story told:
Neither is worth enough to be bought or sold.

Don't think so much about how they feel.
You're at opposite ends of a turning wheel
And neither can either's momentum steal.

CHAPTER 5

Empty space tends to get filled,
Unless its owner becomes skilled
At fending off outsiders' will.

The greatest gift you give is space,
When letting others speak their case
Or letting them know you will wait.

Though it betrays your values, you do -
To keep the peace and make it through,
But this takes an improper toll on you.

The amount of energy you have right now
Is not what yesterday limits or endowed:
It's how ever much you invite and allow.

Yes, it is going to look like obsession
To those in some passionless profession
But this is the path of self-invention.

Though they have quieted to a grumble,
They still sound anything but humble.
Keep composed. Preserve your thunder.

Know your target. Know yourself.
Rely on certainty, not on stealth.
Forget aiming far - just aim well.

This exact same life can be interpreted
As filled with triumph or full of hurt:
It's up to you to decide which works.

The journey is going as it should:
Everything is not always all good,
But more is becoming understood.

Ever since you rounded that corner,
Why has nothing returned to normal?
Because you're on a new way forward.

Do activities that build up your being.
When not busy, find yourself practicing.
Potency is in simple acts of preparing.

This time you have chosen to complicate
Rather than take the way that is straight.
If you cannot see it yet, you should wait.

They will laugh so hard they may fall
When you keep your focus on the small,
Where it's easier to find humor in it all.

A bird cannot move the wind, just each wing
Just as all you can do is each next right thing.
Attention to detail is really all you can bring.

You're marvelous and yet not enough.
You need help from below and above
To accomplish all that must be done.

If they need to complain you should say,
"Now that we know what you need today,
What is best for me is to be on my way."

When you do need to let it out,
Find who knows what you're about
And only then open your mouth.

All of your dealings need to make sense,
Ask that they clarify just what they meant.
All throughout this you should feel content.

You told your truth, there's no more to it.
They'll have to decide how they'll use it.
Your only job is to just keep being fluid.

Help others, but take care of yourself
So you're giving from a place of wealth
With both physical and financial health.

It will be so rare to find an example.
When you do, you'll know if it's ample
By how much it builds or dismantles.

True, you cannot be in both places now,
Though imagination claims it knows how;
So, to this one present you should bow.

One hand builds while the other battles -
Right now, that's just where things are at,
So stay fully aware of each effort's status.

You don't have to fit the normal story.
You don't have to seek standard glory.
You will only have yourself as jury.

No one has come this way yet;
That alone makes you the best
One to know what comes next.

They're wise to as far as they have gone
And past that, can only steer you wrong.
Reposition yourself to where you belong.

What you dream of is just a direction -
Go that way, but keep asking questions.
So you reach not a place, but the lesson.

Have you thought it all the way through?
Is there someone you owe for being you?
Is something outside of you more true?

When flow has to twist around walls,
Somewhere there will be a waterfall.
Therefore, go slowly or not at all.

That was a tunnel that you passed through.
Crowded or twisted, that one's behind you.
Forget about that now and enjoy this view.

There's ease in keeping things the same,
But this is the opposite of why you came:
Change, for change's sake, again and again.

It can be healthy to speak to your sorrow,
But in the wrong group, you'll just wallow:
Do it with others also determined to grow.

With words, speak caringly and sparingly
And use other means to convey unerringly
Whatever needs to be expressed unwarily.

How you talk about that places you in it,
Either as proud owner or griping tenant,
So speak from the role you expect to fit.

So redefine what it could mean to retire.
For some, it is a way to permanently hide.
For you, let it be a way to rest for awhile.

There are no one-size-fits-all methods.
You must be listening to all your senses.
Each says what another didn't mention.

Building back up from where you were
Means you'll have to set up new terms:
Who gets ignored and who gets heard?

Does it fit your set of priorities?
Does it improve your life's quality?
Does it deepen your sense of curiosity?

You are allowed to grieve and sit awhile
But listen closely for the voice inside.
When it says to return, do so in style.

Organize your thoughts. Give this time.
Get them to harmonize, not simply rhyme.
Seek to feel utilized, not simply fine.

When were you last completely quiet?
When did you last attempt to try it?
When will you go on a word diet?

It's good to live by a code for a while,
To focus more on discipline than style,
But quit before your rules merely pile.

You're looking back if you're outrunning.
Better to look up ahead toward something:
You live your best when you're becoming.

Move one step ahead - two if you can.
Get far in front by making your plan,
And then make it the law of your land.

Neither overrate nor downplay this time
All of the work you put in to harmonize
But let your own conclusion materialize.

Let it out, no matter what impedes you.
You must live what you believe is true -
Take the step that brings You into view.

Neither win the future nor beat the past
But completely do today's clearest tasks
And when you can, be thorough, not fast.

You'll be ready, while others hesitate.
You'll get up and get out and navigate.
You'll be the one who sets it straight.

It's not mysterious, complicated or profound:
Sometimes you're up, sometimes you're down.
You need to travel both high and low ground.

It is only important that it is yours,
Not to feel justified in starting wars,
But to be poised to open new doors.

We never lose that which matters to us;
It simply asks us for a new level of trust
When it transcends what can gather dust.

First, do it all the way,
Heading on into the fray,
Willing - come what may.

And how could it have seemed like such fun?
Well-wrapped won't always mean well-done.
Look at all sides - not just the shiniest one.

Trust that an end will arrive.
Your purpose now is to thrive.
Own every bit of being alive.

You are beautiful, despite denying so,
But be mindful - denial is detrimental.
Admitting your beauty is meaningful.

Truly, sometimes some things choose you
Because you are either ready or willing to
Welcome whatever they blossom you into.

Yes, you deserve a moment of pride,
Manifesting all of this from inside;
Now shore up against the downside.

As if you're winning a bet,
Laugh in the face of fret -
Because you're not done yet.

Greet even the most unpleasant surprise.
It is only a gust of wind. You're the sky.
It is only one second. You're all of time.

The trick over time is to entrust more
Of tomorrow to those closer to its door
As you mature into awareness evermore.

It feels wrong to behold suffering.
You feel you ought to be buffering;
Bearing witness is what you bring.

Put it all out there as one body of work.
Put away plans for nexts, lasts and firsts.
Put in the effort until you're immersed.

Consider this a dare to be a beginner again,
To forget all about how, or what, or when,
And just experiment, mess up, play, pretend!

Sometimes, you'll do best to disappear -
Put yourself where you are nowhere near
Influences that would cause you to veer.

How often do you wake up and ask
If it's time to move to the next task?
Get an answer. Press on or turn fast.

Where does your mind travel to soften?
Where does your heart need no caution?
Where do you find yourself most often?

Things either fill space or make room.
What you own should not also own you.
Everything's highest form is servitude.

Not doing is not actually learning -
It is but fountain water, churning;
A stream learns the way by turning.

Your first instinct is correct
So neither retreat nor deflect;
Instead, very closely inspect.

There is something deeper going on,
Something you need to put focus on,
Before you stay here too long.

Activities are not what get it done -
Aligning, like a blossom toward the sun
Is how an easeful life should be run.

They have certainly brought you abundance
Of what you want or else your comeuppance;
Gratefully accept this or risk redundance.

You shouldn't be there. You should go.
Moving ahead without so much in tow.
Be bold. Dig deep and just say so.

Look at what's smiling back at you.
Look at its beauty as physical proof:
Look at how love is looking at you.

It is fine for them to ask it of you.
It is fine for you to do all of it too.
It is also fine for you to just refuse.

Clarity needs ample room to see true, so
Stay unattached from all points of view.
Free of a plan you will know what to do.

You tried to be clear, which wasn't enough.
Your time needs more than a nurturing love;
Today it needs you to be stubborn and tough.

When people do things that are just mean,
You're just the lucky one caught in between
Where you're going and where they've been.

Trust your gut - your wordless instinct,
Your sage giving teachings most succinct.
Thanks be to the way that you're linked.

Savor times between wanting and getting.
They're when you see what you're letting
Jam up your present by never forgetting.

Incompetence can show up anywhere.
And taunt you? It will certainly dare.
Trap it in your most all-seeing stare.

There is nothing you need to cut loose.
There is no solution for you to deduce.
There are only paths for you to choose.

Can you finally forget about the how?
To synchronicity can you finally bow?
Open and observe, appreciate and allow.

Sometimes people stink - we just do.
And once you figure out it's not you,
You can go around to sniff out who.

Thoughts that make you breathe easily
Point in the direction of your destiny
And just as deeply, change everything.

Wherever your hand goes in conversation
Points toward where you keep hesitation:
Focus your inner work on this location.

Even with both feet planted on the ground,
Your spirit can be felt, traveling all around
As you treasure all the people you've found.

You need to inhabit this space above all
And let other activities around you fall
Away as you rise, stretch and stand tall.

What came before helps you produce
Just as buds bloom thanks to roots;
You will be something's basis too.

Expectation can stifle joy. Be mindful.
Explanation can go unending. Be final.
Everything but love can go. Be primal.

They have even more ways to get you upset
You've been dealing with them but instead
Try new tactics they would never suspect.

When it's time, everything gets left behind
So practice right now within your own mind
By letting some defining memories unbind.

There is a world far beyond being liked,
Where you uncover more than you might
Once you put their opinions out of sight.

All this effort you are prepared to use
Should instead go to help you to choose
Which of your stories it's time to lose.

Lumping these all together is incorrect.
To split those up could be to disrespect.
So weigh what your decision will affect.

Regardless of which option you choose,
There is something within what you do
That invites an energy to flow through.

At some point, your feelings won't matter:
You'll simply lose interest in their patterns
Though you may still patiently have them.

This is an invitation to yet one more
Uncharted location for you to explore.
If you are willing, much is in store.

The true power of each thought
Was not in doing what it ought,
But in what all else it brought.

It angers you because of what it triggers,
Not because it points out anything bigger:
What you need to do is to disarm quicker.

CHAPTER 6

You will come across it everywhere else
So why not start right here with yourself?
Work solely on your own highest health.

If you can pick one thing let it be sleep
Since the right amount satisfies the need
For your spirit to enjoy a full renewing.

At some point the habit must stop.
Lay down tonight and just let it drop
And awaken a little lighter on top.

There's not much left to talk about -
Give them space to protest and pout.
Stay inwardly still. Throw them out.

Ask yourself, before you say yes -
Not whether one decision is best -
But how it will benefit the next.

Close the books filled with old stories,
Because not even the very best of these
Can top your own unfolding mysteries.

It's not a sign of greed, but of wealth,
An abundance of both love and health
To take ever better care of yourself.

Life has added on one thing more,
Not to give you yet another chore,
But to show you yet another door.

The choice is not between this or that,
But between your path and a given track;
One's forever forward, the other, back.

If you can see confusion up ahead, turn.
Chaos leads one way - straight to a burn.
Closer to harmony, it's easier to learn.

Setting aside time to care for yourself last
Should become an ugly habit of your past.
Self-care can be a way of living, not a task.

When it is right, there is no knowing,
No trial with evidence to be showing -
Only a feeling that just keeps growing.

You'll have to collaborate with someone else
Because you should go no further by yourself
To guard and grow your own overall health.

A challenge that makes you feel queasy
Need not be gnawed on until it is easy;
Feed it to one who can enjoy it deeply.

Say whatever must be said - but kindly.
The mind opens when dealt with wisely.
Words work best when delivered mildly.

What lifts your feet up off of the floor?
When does joy well up from your core?
How could you enjoy this forevermore?

Thoughts come from, and turn into feelings.
So the situation with which you're dealing
Can help you think your way into healing.

So much is perfect the way things are -
You should inhale before raising the bar:
Enjoy what's close before traveling far.

Just reach out toward that direction
And begin to sense their intention:
You know beyond what's mentioned.

For all your doubts to be depleted
And your heart to feel completed,
You may need the lesson repeated.

You were just there - in your natural state -
In the place that you neither rush nor wait,
And where you are neither small nor great.

It is time to reach out to other ones
Who can help you get much more done -
And show you what you find most fun.

It makes sense that you have fewer peers:
It means you've made yourself very clear
For the right ones to come find you here.

Right now, what are your priorities?
When we look into each one of these
Which ones stir both drive and ease?

Listen to yourself, but not too closely
To the inner chatter talking mostly:
It is just a guest - you are hosting.

Keep them at a distance if they delay.
Keep them farther if their efforts sway.
Keep them close if they are underway.

Interrupt whoever drudges up history.
Politely redirect talk of dark mystery.
Mind all that travels conversationally.

No need to refuse out of spite,
But if they wasted your advice
How will they treat your time?

Slowing you down may be what they need,
But slow down at your own chosen speed.
You won't need to be moving to proceed.

Though this was not a part of your plan,
It doesn't mean that you can't. You can.
Goals, like water should flow, not stand.

They are now far yet still feel very dear,
But you need to focus yourself right here
So you can both be heard as well as hear.

Find a good friend and tell it to them;
Hear how it sounds and then notice when
They ask you to say what you said again.

Life has a way of always getting better
If you follow this advice to the letter:
See goodness in every season's weather.

One way or the other, you are an example
Either by letting your reactions trample
Or taking steps that are lovingly ample.

You'll find out by being open to anything.
Be open to anything by expecting nothing,
And expect nothing by loving everything.

You will soar once you let yourself plummet.
Study the stories of people who have done it -
Gone into the unknown to launch far above it.

Living is only ever about how you feel:
Though motivations are easily concealed,
They are all your mind regards as real.

Or don't prepare at all; Just improvise
If you find it too foreign to visualize
But try to have some feel of the prize.

You possess more strength than you realize,
More healing power than a hospital inside,
More wealth than could ever be monetized.

You have done well to not get roped in,
But before you declare an official win,
Look well at what next thing you begin.

You handled it well, whether you realize yet.
You were so natural, with no agendas preset -
This is the best way to live free from regret.

You are allowed to build a prison of rage.
You are also allowed to pry open that cage.
You are also allowed to be an everyday sage.

Intensity feels fine for awhile,
But soon enough goes out of style.
Try out something that runs mild.

You have woken up inside this circumstance
That looks like anything but another chance,
But your abilities are about to be enhanced.

It's time to measure what you've done -
It's not the same as measuring outcome:
Measure out what you've actually begun.

It is important to be right where you are
Whether or not you feel you've gotten far
Because you need this in your repertoire.

When you hear people complain about time,
How they're managing theirs isn't right,
So do the opposite and more you'll find.

Once you are done wanting and getting
Come to the place of intention-setting
Manifesting more in living by letting.

It is alright to invite a little drama
If it can be for your sentence a comma
And not drag on into an endless saga.

Don't go down that road. Stay on this one.
It is better-maintained and gets more sun,
Which helps whether you walk, jog or run.

You have thought all this through before
So trust in yourself and revisit no more;
Build up with all of that as your floor.

Stop wondering what anyone else thinks.
In your plan that will make some kinks.
Opinion gets stale and then it stinks.

How much easier it is when you have more help.
How much easier it is when you welcome wealth.
How much easier it is when you position yourself.

You need to say that's enough,
That this road is plenty rough
Without hotheads flaring up.

You can predict what's going to happen
Based on all of their previous actions,
So you already know just what to fasten.

You have to start with nothing
To understand this one thing:
You are what you're becoming.

You might not be at peace with your past
Until you reframe those circumstances as
Your life birthing itself through chance.

To some, you are the utmost authority
On thinking about patterns creatively.
Be proud of this and live accordingly.

When you want to stand up and run
In order to get everything all done,
Forget about the many for the one.

There was no path from which to stray,
No charted route to sail through today
Because you are both wayfinder and way.

You are here not to flee, but to chase,
But not like running a planned-out race;
You are here to catch up to open space.

Ignore how it feels right now - continue
Because what you've gotten yourself into
Points to what you are truly here to do.

Rough self-motivation is just as rude as
A teacher shouting the lesson in school.
Loving-kindness is more powerful fuel.

It's a story that used to trigger you,
But you know what you need to do.
You're able to see straight through.

Your defiance in the face of the storm
Is a noble yet misdirected venture, for
It comes, not to surprise, but to warn.

Go numb to all the phenomena
That come and are then gone;
Feel for what goes on and on.

Sometimes your preference is irrelevant.
Sometimes you're the branch to be bent.
Sometimes you're the message to be sent.

The numbers will either grow or shrink
Without telling you about a deeper link
Between how to live and how you think.

Say goodbye to unchosen feelings.
Free of them, no longer kneeling,
You are sheer lightness of being.

Take as long as you need to come to peace
To the spot where inner accusations cease
And things don't bother you in the least.

When you put your hand over your core,
It means you're guarding against more.
Of what? Answering is your next chore.

What challenges you offers you a choice;
Realize the reason you're given a voice
Is to speak sense that quiets the noise.

This may be the time for you to be brave
And stand for yourself and others today.
Be here rooted in truth, come what may.

Your place must be closer to the action -
Not for money, fame or even satisfaction -
But for the removal of every distraction.

Remember that this is only a projection
Of your thoughts and more so intentions
Even the ones you prefer not to mention.

So your want doesn't turn to greed,
Before you get what you truly need
Go do for someone else a good deed.

Keep your head down. Work on your craft,
Close the workshop door. Let in no draft.
You need to be driven - not well-staffed.

Most of them won't matter at all,
But one key detail is invaluable -
The one that feels least repeatable.

The art of living shows in your wit
So if you can, try to laugh about it
And invite everyone to giggle a bit.

Hear this: your beauty is in your limits -
So instead of seeking mentors to mimic,
Pay your precious vulnerabilities a visit.

Your body requested the right remedy
And hopes you paid attention especially
By silencing that know-it-all tendency.

This is the time to look it in the face,
To be duly firm, to put it in its place,
To embody power that embodies grace.

Just like flowers, people can grow,
The same way any seed can be sown -
With care given and patience shown.

Connection is an added benefit,
But that is not why you did this:
Stay close to what inspired it.

Does your destination still feel true?
Is it where your heart is leading you?
Is it close enough to be within view?

All boundaries do is wait to be crossed
(owners of fences still get distraught).
Out past boundaries, get happily lost.

No one's going to show you the right way
Ask the supposed experts though you may;
This is one part of the price you must pay.

All your tasks contribute to your goal,
Provided you can do them from the soul.
So tell them they are part of the whole.

Who can say how things will go?
You already know: no one knows.
You can only choose to grow.

It's wonderful to be a self-starter,
But refusing help makes it harder
Than flowing together like water.

Mind what you let your thoughts think
Because of how all those thoughts link;
Not all water is meant for you to drink.

For the new things you needed to know
How many old did you need to let go?
Do you allow for the ebb and flow?

Go face the source of all this confusion,
Through each of its fine veils of illusion
And bring this chapter to its conclusion.

Health isn't an investment; it's a way.
Forget tomorrow's benefits - notice today
How a bit of exercise helps your brain.

If you look around and see a mess,
It means your routine is in distress
And needs you to do one thing less.

How would you need to be? So become that
Even if it requires you to wear many hats
Until you learn how to be where you're at.

Go ahead - if you're full of curiosity -
Go see who fate would like you to meet.
Go if it's less a task and more a treat.

Do you do the same thing over and over?
And has it made you any faster or slower?
Most importantly: do you feel any closer?

Do you worry that you'll sound too weird?
Or that you are precisely what they feared?
Head straight - your way has been cleared.

As heart cannot be mind,
Giving must not be blind:
Leave cluelessness behind.

CHAPTER 7

Have a kind of clarity that stands guard
So that it makes a fence round your yard
And other things will no longer be hard.

You must be done with correcting others;
Passion breathes but correcting smothers
Via revisions the sentiment of Another.

Take what's needed, give back the rest
Just like taking air into your chest;
The rule is that enough is what's best.

The feelings will go and you will stay.
So be with what you know to be underway
And allow everything, including a delay.

Look again at how things are laid out;
Do they reflect what you're all about?
Is everything set in the right amount?

This is still a time of transition;
Whatever seems out of position
Is just slow to obey your wishes.

What if you made it work just for you?
When being selfish you can find truth.
When you are satisfied, others are too.

What you do may sound very interesting
To others, but do you find it riveting?
If so, perfect. If not, start pivoting.

The memories help when times are tough
But reminiscing because today is rough,
Misses the fact that here now is enough.

Keep believing in being clear
For that is what keeps you here
And draws the best things near.

You're overloaded. You're thinking to excess.
From another angle, see how you are blessed
To even have such reasons to get stressed.

Enough of the items - on to the action;
For planning brings far less satisfaction
Than genuine, meaningful interaction.

What is it you do to make them furious?
Aren't you more than just a bit curious?
Are they rightly concerned or delirious?

Choose a little bit more consciously
So that whatever you may be deciding
Matches up with some deeper belief.

How it is isn't worth complaining about,
Spend one full hour mapping another route
And then pack your gear and then set out.

This is a time to bear down and tackle
This problem that so many has baffled.
Between both worlds you must straddle.

Dream before dawn and do before dusk,
This is the life you've chosen and must
Honor what elders in you did entrust.

Whatever story appears to be rising
Is something all of you were writing
To act out together. Come out of hiding.

Temper is the most accurate indicator
Of what you already put off until later
And has grown into something greater.

Are the rules necessary, or convenient?
Do they cheer you on or watch, silent?
Can you tell which ones are irrelevant?

As long as you're trying to get somewhere
You'll meet people with things to compare;
Be right here - all that's left to do is share.

Give out compliments; wait for none back.
Whether as words or thoughts, you attract
Adoration in too many ways to keep track.

Can you recognize what makes you whole?
When with others, do you feed your soul?
Will you discover truth past being told?

Your body has spoken, so do not delay.
It keeps telling you in its gentlest way
That what is within can no longer stay.

The desire to take this risk,
And whatever it comes with,
Is the most important shift.

It is never too early nor too late
To build something that resonates:
Someone somewhere sincerely waits.

Receiving an unpleasant offer
Will train you never to waffle
Declining all except awesome.

Gifts can get thrown out unintentionally
Unless we decide to sort conscientiously
What belongs inside versus on the heap.

Control isn't why you're here.
Events are not yours to steer.
Be light and open and clear.

Body and brain both need exercise
To keep you healthy as well as wise;
Work with each based on its size.

Of the powers beyond your understanding,
You should be eager, but never demanding
To learn from each how to keep expanding.

Check the way you're talking to yourself:
Better words raise your lifetime's wealth.
Better tones raise your heartbeat's health.

To connect around discussing problems
Might not actually help you solve them:
Spend your time discussing knowledge.

Do your thing, needing to join no group
That may dilute the flavor of your soup
Or borrow time you'll need to recoup.

Most of this is out of your control,
So remember to let go of your role
Because you are both young and old.

It is as foolish to blame your reflection
For a blemish you see in its complexion
As it is to find the fault in the tension.

Whether your paperwork compares,
Your experience surpasses theirs
So don't be unruly, but be aware.

Your thoughts recreate what you see,
So you must put yourself accordingly
Where you find both effort and ease.

When you are done, it will just be shed;
When other things interest you instead,
Not a bit will dwell inside your head.

At this point, you're already halfway.
No one's opinion is welcome today -
Just get through all that's underway.

You have not had even one enemy,
Just people who showed painfully
All that you needed to see: So see.

No matter who tries to get you to move,
You have to stick to your own values.
All you have is your power to choose.

Looking at the effort you've exerted,
Has this made you even more certain?
Do you see another door you can open?

Putting positivity into every word said
Signals gossip's vultures high overhead
To flap elsewhere for the dying or dead.

This is not the time or place for focus.
It is the time to find space to be open
To make sense of all that's unfolded.

You don't always have to be smiling
Or to be clever, quick or beguiling;
You should share what's underlying.

Achieve the things to know how that feels,
Then pause to reflect on what you have seen
And you will understand what it all means.

Adding one more thing takes something away
From letting things be what they are today -
Filling up emptiness leads your focus astray.

There is more wisdom than you can imagine.
You have experienced just a mere fraction;
The rest needs more discussion to happen.

Let your expectations die away lovingly.
Let it be enough to exchange the energy.
Let renewed senses transmit and receive.

If you let your thoughts linger here,
You'll train them in a loop to steer;
Decide and let it be perfectly clear.

Uncomfortable putting your name out there?
If it doesn't go on your work, then where?
Put your name on it to show that you care.

Change is taking its own sweet time,
But it is coming as you will soon find,
So stay flexibly strong, body and mind.

Take time for your own sake, take time.
Down the long road awaits the sublime.
Your impact is a poem; you are one line.

You made the decision to shift.
You don't need to create a list.
You get to decide, then insist.

What question is content with one reply?
What question does not somehow multiply?
What question are you willing to let die?

And why did you need to go over there?
Why did you believe you needed repair?
Can you flow with flaws and not care?

While it's best not to assume malintent
Sometimes subtle harm is what was meant;
As if a landlord, do not let them rent.

It's as simple to say as this:
"What once did, no longer fits."
Everything changes. Everything shifts.

Inviting so much noise into your core
Is not what the act of inviting is for -
Add a step between meeting and more.

Sometimes the delivery has to stink
To get you to stop staring and blink
So you can reset yourself and think.

Rather than getting yourself uptight,
â—‹Know you're not here to get it right:
You are here to sharpen your insight.

The child in you is what is wonderful,
Curing seriousness by being whimsical.
Let more out because it's truly magical.

Powers must ultimately be combined,
And the tricky part in joining minds
Is freeing them yet making them bind.

Enjoyment, comfort - these aren't enough
To be your complete expression of love.
You are Everything, not a part thereof.

You'll assume you've been here before,
The familiar faces and feelings galore.
It's a misjudgment you should ignore.

Some people say things that truly hurt
That make you feel as low down as dirt
Which is where growth awaits rebirth.

When you get the chance, ask all you can.
Let your imagination in their place stand.
Let their experience help refine your plan.

There are things you still need to know,
Waiting around that corner in the road.
Let this be reason enough for you to go.

What they see is only a delayed reflection:
Where you were, not where you're headed.
You do not owe them their misconception.

How are you viewing it? Solely from here?
Have you looked down from the atmosphere?
And let your imagination see everywhere?

There's no need to clamor for more
All will be delivered to your door;
Go to it then - not a moment before.

Use what you gain to let something go;
What is overgrown has no room to grow.
Your inner landscape could use a mow.

Overstimulated minds and toddlers whine.
So unplug from it all from time to time.
We each have a child to parent inside.

Lasting changes arrive in odd packages
So when receiving, the best practice is
To be as open to gifts as to challenges.

Your surroundings will limit your ideas
Until you decide to be extremely clear
About who you are and why you're here.

As convincing as other methods may be
They're all just volumes in your library
You're now doing, not just researching.

Help those who help themselves
For the complaining it dispels
And the momentum it compels.

Forward no matter what. Tell yourself again.
Forget about how far until you reach the end.
Decide you will go, with or without friends.

Time always reveals more, so just wait.
Have a lifetime view; you can't be late.
You see turns, but the way is straight.

A situation becomes harder out of context;
A vision will keep you from getting vexed
So keep picturing what should come next.

Whatever your age, seek out an elder,
A time-tested mentor, a genuine helper
To build you an experience-based shelter.

Until they break their cycle of depression,
Quarantine yourself from that connection
And disinfect all your internal questions.

You do not need to know much more;
Come here, behold yourself and adore
The one who exceeds what was before.

Your mind is so sure you need to act,
But it has not gotten all of the facts:
What you can do is take a step back.

Sometimes you can't escape the tangle,
So position yourself at a strategic angle
And rally everyone you need to wrangle.

Use patient ears to hear negative words.
Someone is trying to convey their hurt.
Open heart, toward love and light turn.

Be mindful of the urge to relax.
It can lead too far to get back,
And there you'll be - off track.

When exploring, don't cut your own path:
Duck, bend and turn. Make your way past
What may be landmarks for the way back.

When did you last refuse the traditional?
So go do something wholly unpredictable:
For your heart, it will be truly medicinal.

Your greatest treasure is your time.
It is the only treasure you may find
By looking as far ahead as behind.

You've done enough. That was the end.
If they come back to invite you again,
Show that on this, you will not bend.

Trust the hints that you are receiving.
Though words and acts can be deceiving,
Your body grants the truth of feeling.

Doesn't have to be fought, fixed or forced -
There is a reason. This thing has a source.
Relax and you'll see and say, "Of course!"

What you assume is well-meaning
Is preventing you from varying:
Be willing to change everything.

Understand when you speak, there's an energy
That reaches out far more than just mentally
And abides in the hearer's heart's memory.

You aren't the one who made that mess
So back away from the chaos and stress
And tend to the task of your own nest.

Now is not the time to look for a limit,
Or hunt for unnecessary things to omit;
It is time to inhale and expand into it.

Everyone is traveling somewhere special,
So if you can't help to speed their vessel,
At least help them keep to their schedule.

Just in case you refused to accept
Lessons that were meant to be kept,
A refresher course is coming next.

CHAPTER 8

There'll be no problem you cannot solve
If you open your heart to forever evolve:
Watch all you let go of simply dissolve.

You don't know what you're getting into
When you begin. You're just not meant to.
So look for the questions, and hints too.

If more of this will keep things the same,
Then the one decision to make is to change
Both your approach as well as your aim.

And now open your hands for all to see
That you've shared with them everything
And that now they must all let you be.

Why you pick the things you do
Is as important as how you do.
Yes, why not always improve?

Don't get addicted to people's trust
Or start telling yourself you must;
Fixed thinking, like old iron, rusts.

Small decisions have the biggest effects,
With greatness or not, each one connects,
So create a schedule your mind respects.

When you're on either side of that feud,
Whether called "hero" or not, you lose
Unless and until you do as you choose.

You're on the brink of a great big shift
By choosing what feels good and uplifts.
Entire destinies change just like this.

Time for you to leave this place,
To compete in that bigger race,
To look your Power in its face.

The whole thing has to go like this:
Even if it happens to be inaccurate,
You keep trying until something fits.

You don't need to finish - simply start.
Love is in love with your lovely heart.
Connecting is the most important part.

Accidentally saying what's impossible
Sheds light on something meaningful -
That limits are absolutely reversible.

Expectations are weeds - clip them back.
Garden well, and what threatens, attack.
Uproot each and every sprout of a lack.

So their issue becomes no greater
Handle it now - there is no later.
Your path could be no straighter.

Your intentions are supposed to change
As experience gives you a wider range.
Revisit what you want again and again.

Rather than feeling the need to worry,
It will make more sense to just hurry
And finish it all in a fantastic flurry.

If you will work, you will not be denied.
Even if the weather decides to be unkind,
Don't be among those who sigh, "I tried."

Be in it from a place of stillness.
Set your own time and noise limits.
Live a longer-lasting fulfillment.

Where you get stuck, take special note:
This is where there's no room for rote,
You will become the expert they quote.

You know a thing is far from dead
When you see its skin being shed;
Is your discomfort being misread?

Do you understand and uphold your worth?
Value your background, in fact, do this first.
Know your price like a farmer knows earth.

    What may sound like a rough delivery
    Is your latest lesson's outer packaging
    Well worth whatever inconveniencing.

    Change is only necessary if you say so;
    Staying the same brings benefits also -
    Like learning how to maintain a flow.

    To keep the crowds out of your garden,
    Post up signs, implore visitors' pardon
    To not step where you've worked hardest.

    You come, you go; you shed, you grow.
    Only in darkness can you see it glow:
    A star in the direction you must go.

Whatever you cling to should go out next
To put your comfort zone to the test and
See with or without, you remain blessed.

    The first try cannot be perfect.
    But what can be is the attempt -
    So focus only on each next step.

Sometimes none of it will make any sense
And you'll have to decide which elements
You're going to acknowledge as relevant.

See this from that other point of view.
It's not absurd, it's simply new to you.
If you were them you would do it too.

How will you know it is time to move on?
When that daily unpredictability is gone.
You need to keep moving to stay strong.

Keep up with changes in your body,
Gauging your strength and flexibility
Because they decide tomorrow's ease.

The ones who fret are constantly plotting,
Rooted in all of their conspiracy-spotting.
Outgrow them so fast you need repotting.

Go ahead call it dark - call it so lonely
The whole point is that this is the only
Set of stairs up to your innermost holy.

When you slip up, fate will tease
By snatching away the joy of ease,
Until you organize and say please.

You can't learn this one soon enough:
Life starts when you stop doing stuff
And is loveliest when you won't rush.

Love yourself and you'll see another way
One that you overlooked just yesterday -
One that would serve well come what may.

You have barely reached halfway,
So now that it's half underway,
You can do things more your way.

What caused that inconvenience?
Was it a lack of self-obedience?
Or the need for a little lenience?

Being who you are is being nothing else
Except that which makes it clear to tell
That you honor yourself by living well.

If you won't listen to praise directly,
You're blocking things from connecting;
Gratitude is all about being accepting.

Almost as soon as you set up a standard,
That one request will become a demand.
But keep your mind on the task at hand.

Put it off for as long as you need to,
But eventually you must tell the truth
About what is no longer in you to do.

Have you ever been wrong before?
Did you end up finding out more?
Isn't that what you're here for?

There is no straight line,
Except the passage of time
To help clarify and refine.

The new way awaits your certain say-so,
Which comes once you head-to-toe know
It is solely about imagining your flow.

Places where people steal from one another
Remind you to get yourself out from under
Anyone who views generosity as a blunder.

This is your journey of self-expression
That from outside looks like obsession
But is answering your life's question.

There is a difference between the two -
Not in the talents you need to use, but
In the energy you need to redistribute.

Set times you don't wish to be disturbed.
If interrupted, repeat until you're heard,
"Be disappointed. I will not be stirred."

It's not about checking off things on a list.
It's about being open enough for each shift
So life can keep on bringing you its gifts.

Delay your gratification and get back to it.
Or let enjoyment lay in pushing through.
Know that in this you are among the few.

Your habits are as waves in your ocean,
Keeping everything you start in motion,
Drowning out every unproductive notion.

What you're doing is sowing the seed,
Tomorrow's steadfast and fruitful tree
That'll sprout, spread, shade and feed.

Don't think of everyone - focus on a few.
And of them, only the small fraction who
You can directly talk and deeply listen to.

The time for celebrating has moved on -
Not to say that to relax would be wrong,
But it's time to do what keeps you strong.

And now you are going to have to trust
Because if you are to keep on rising up,
Learning goes from a should to a must.

If you dislike paying this high price,
Realize that the price is exactly right
For the lesson all of this holds inside.

There are so many ways to get there
That you can take any. But beware -
Halfway is the quickest to nowhere.

You are so beautiful, you needn't try,
A beauty even visible to blind eyes,
A beauty that has already arrived.

Study as many mistakes as you can gather,
Or live them firsthand if you would rather;
Each one adds a rung to your life's ladder.

What are you waiting for?
Someone to give you more?
What have you already stored?

Reach a sense of where is your limit -
Of what you can give and then give it;
This is how you meet with your spirit.

When all the inputs start to overwhelm,
Remember you are a captain at the helm
Able to sail toward any chosen realm.

You are vital to us all, regardless -
Whether you pursue external success
Or choose to remain here and bless.

There is no one, single, ideal way;
There is only your intention today,
Which may be best to write, not say.

These attempts you've made are just that -
None a final version - each one is a draft,
Or a sketching, but not the finished map.

Time now to decide what you want to see
Of the world and who you're ready to be
Because you have enough to do anything.

What you don't question picks at you
To pry your weakest assumption loose
So reevaluate your whole way through.

In food and fitness, spend generously.
Be well through these - not medically.
You will benefit more than physically.

Regardless of either luck or labor,
Regardless of coming now or later,
It will all work out in your favor.

It can be frustrating to be in need,
But just imagine how an infant feels
And trust that growth is guaranteed.

No need to begrudge the road behind you,
But do tighten any wheels that came loose;
Out of everything try to get the most use.

A habit might help you forget to grow
By praising you for just staying aglow
But you can burn brighter, you know.

You need to know just enough to begin,
But not so much you won't head on in:
You'll learn to sail once there is wind.

Is any of it moving backwards?
Are there far too many factors?
What one thing truly matters?

You don't need their love - you need yours
To welcome them in, or open closed doors.
You need a love that comes from your core.

Once you are standing up in this fully,
Details will no longer be able to bully
(Everything makes way for certainty).

It becomes pointless to remain on guard,
Because the answer was never that hard:
Step out of your own mind's backyard.

Maybe later you can look at it again.
For now, it needs to come to an end.
Right now, if you're not sure when.

Showing your temper may have one benefit:
It will shift the tone from falsely delicate
And force the focus onto what is relevant.

A chapter closes before the next begins
Whether or not you found it interesting;
Not everything important is riveting.

Exactly why does it need to be so huge?
Is your thirst only quenched by deluge?
How much of it all will your heart use?

Stop talking to those who fuss and rage,
Rattling against their own imagined cage.
Nurture a peace that surpasses your age.

When you need to ingrain better patterns
To maintain focus on what truly matters,
Light the way with love as your lantern.

Invite the energy that a new one brings.
Let your competition birth great things,
One collaboration gives ideas two wings.

You be the one who decides your beliefs.
Think about every single thing you read.
Be a pupil for only as long as you need.

For now, just find out a little bit more
So that you build on a foundation sure
Something that will work and endure.

Whether or not you feel on the verge,
Sooner or later the truth will emerge
With more spontaneity than an urge.

It will be better to focus on quality
Of a kind you can touch, hear and see
So you can live deep within integrity.

To live for the future is to live a lie,
And the past is a life you must let die.
If this isn't obvious only you know why.

Including today's mood too,
How is your overall attitude?
Should you refresh or renew?

And sometimes it takes one huge push,
A grueling effort, a send-off, a whoosh,
If your Will were a sled dog, a "Mush!"

As gardening must tend to the soil below,
Know when to say yes and when to say no.
To make success that much easier to grow.

Gather up treasures as you journey along
So that even though your journey be long,
You will only become increasingly strong.

In the face of the upcoming unknown,
Know coincidences can help you grow
As you let what is to be simply unroll.

Invite your newest friendships gradually.
Take time, to perceive things accurately
So when you know, you know actually.

Given the insight you now know to use,
Each of your senses can also help choose
The way that holds your greatest truths.

Be firm, don't let anyone dissuade you.
Your decision was key, and made through
A steady, unshakable willingness to do.

Your difficulties are not all dreamed up;
The uninvited are drinking from your cup
And need you to tell them that's enough.

CHAPTER 9

When it's right, everything easily flows.
When it's right, everyone already knows
Because you embody it from top to toes.

Start that next piece before this one is done
And if your mind keeps asking for a reason:
Nothing can finish until after you've begun.

There are so many ways to interpret all this.
There are so many ways to make yourself fit.
There is only one way to authentically live.

A mind on the task and a heart on hand
Will ensure you are doing all you can
To help some fly and let others land.

Have you been told before?
You don't need to do more:
Your delivery opens doors.

Go and get the best tools,
Learn all the basic rules,
Excel in your own school.

It is all about the words that you use;
Everything else just serves to confuse.
Expression is beautiful from any view.

Hard work is pointless labor
Until your reason is greater,
And then the impact is major.

You are not here for idle chitchat -
But to go where today's truth is at:
Be the listener - not the diplomat.

You need to let them pass you by
Because you're headed far outside
The realm that they came to find.

Most important to keep in mind is why
So that when you are asked to decide,
You are already so perfectly aligned.

What we accomplish matters little,
Goals alone are fleeting and brittle;
Make this day a poem, not a riddle.

What sort of role do you have to wear?
Are you expected to have a certain air?
Is it something you give proper care?

Put that down. You need to be learning.
You need to keep your interest churning.
What's obsolete you need to be burning.

The sun will certainly beam once more,
You will bloom even better than before.
Thank the darkness and what it was for.

You already know this, yet still drift:
Self-care is not optional on your list.
It is the only way to unwrap this gift.

Who knows how this may end up turning out?
Whoever claims to has less mind than mouth.
What always works is to water what sprouts.

Start budgeting either money or time
And the other will immediately align
As your accounting continues to refine.

Think of a time when you lost your voice
And see if you had already made a choice
To silence your inner expressing of joy.

There's nothing for you back there anymore.
So instead use this time to relax and restore,
Because today has for you adventures galore.

And while they are sharing their worry,
Permit your mind to go off on a journey
To anywhere else and return in no hurry.

You have known what it is to be in pain.
You give help when others feel the same.
For this, people are speaking your name.

Rushing makes it all seem and feel fake,
So use all the time that it needs to take
For yours, its, and everyone else's sake.

Be very strict about what you allow
Your mind to think - and also how.
Build later. Gather your tools now.

Now close that door that is still ajar -
There's plenty to do here where you are
And you are the most qualified by far.

Your creation should never ask for change
From those who need that to stay the same.
Do this for those who also have your aim.

If you would do what you enjoy for free,
Then why not for everyone simultaneously?
Expand your concept of how far you reach.

Why are you this upset?
This irked, this vexed?
Give love to this next.

Whoever claims they've things to teach,
Do they know what you desire to reach?
Is there proof of what they can unleash?

Sleep on it - let one good night of rest help
Your whole decision-making process go well
By bringing you back to your original self.

Truly, and first of all, love what you do.
But right behind that, own all of it, too.
This is how to design a life built for you.

You don't get to perfect everything at once,
Nor can an animal pick several things to hunt
If it wants to catch what it leaps to confront.

You were lied to, and now know the truth:
Could that discovery create someone new?
It can't - it's just data: now calmly choose.

The way you express your joy is healing
Especially when your laughter is peeling
You away from every unpleasant feeling.

No one else has to agree.
No one even needs to see.
Everyone must let you be.

Hiding in shadows as their survival habit,
Scavengers find what they can and grab it
Far from the brightness that you inhabit.

What can you sculpt on a finished statue?
Without hardship, what's left to react to?
In plainer words, no challenge, no value.

When you want to just turn around
Or sit right here on the ground,
Allow yourself to be found.

Become better at knowing the way back
Because when you find yourself off track
You need only draw upon workable facts.

What you really need to understand
Is that giving your heart and hand
Also means giving up all demands.

Who's around you reflects what's within.
So look to the Chooser before you begin
To judge anyone - friend, enemy, or kin.

If you were asked about your intention,
Would your answer also include mention
Of your living in that same direction?

It's not that you shouldn't care what they think -
You cannot know what pushes them to the brink,
So why not just make yourself the farthest link?

Whether you realize it or not,
This is exactly what you want:
You can decide what to drop.

Bravely will make the safest way there.
Those in hiding will hide and not dare
Because of your certain, confident air.

Do you think of the end when you begin?
Do you lead with your nose or your chin?
What comes out is based on what went in.

Being asked to do yet more can be flattering,
But your time is not paint to be splattering.
You have to return to what's truly mattering.

You must trust in more than yourself
Both to strengthen your mental health
And expand your definition of wealth.

This time, yes, you need to vent
Both for all that it will prevent
And for the release it represents.

The words don't even have to be hostile
To upend your sensibilities for a while
But reorient and go get back your smile.

We only think we know what we need
So the thing to do is look between
How it is and how it's perceived.

Yes, appreciate all the beautiful things!
But also notice what the ordinary brings.
Are you the song or the one who sings?

They will be cleared out of your way
Once you learn they are here to stay
And it's you who needs to turn away.

Some lift you up and some wear you down;
Those who tend to leave you with a frown
Are telling you to go tread new ground.

Perhaps the best part about a second try
Is that you get to focus entirely on why
And really get to know the inner guide.

That wasn't the way you prefer to hear it,
But it couldn'tve been painted any clearer:
You are not the doer - you're the hearer.

There doesn't have to be a reason why.
You just have to decide to and then try;
A bird doesn't question when in-flight.

Feelings may cause you to do worse
Than if you stood back from it first
To notice who is acting out of hurt.

Keep yourself a little bit unsatisfied,
With something still irking your pride,
So that when you roar, fear will hide.

Usually when you think you've lost it all,
Something else happens to prove you wrong:
Giving thanks will always keep you strong.

There are times for taking risks,
And then times for making shifts.
You already know which this is.

Did you drag the past this far?
Can you postpone the memoir?
Will you forget who you are?

You know what you know when you know it
Before nor After have anywhere to stow it
Once you are at peace with this, show it.

Let everyone else stay at the festival -
For you, let that be incomprehensible
As you train to become your best of all.

With this fuller idea of who you are,
You will see the path ahead quite far
With the help of some familiar stars.

An uplifting friendship is best of all;
It comes to find you whenever you fall
And goes on reminding you to stand tall.

Your role is to simply start the legacy,
To be the first who helps others to see
That giving is the best way to succeed.

If you say this is the last time,
You'd better be ready to be fine
With crossing a different line.

The kind of preparation you favor
Isn't what you need now or later -
Build a space for you as Creator.

It is uncomfortable to overextend
But you must, to see yourself bend
To break what's brittle at each end.

If someone is certain they are in crisis
Little you'll do to turn them from this.
Do not address what they claim's amiss.

For what it's worth, keep holding on
Even though the thrill may seem gone
Thoughts of brightness bring the dawn.

We're born, we grow, we bloom, we go.
For exactly how long, no being knows.
Time aside, we all came here to glow.

Clarity can end up coming soon
If you take time to make room,
Which seals confusion's tomb.

It is not about some one thing you do -
It's about your honesty coming through
By putting aside your how for your who.

It is time to be more than an observer.
It is time for you to go even further -
Into what inspires your deepest fervor.

Despite what the resentful are whining,
The greatest impact is all about timing:
Keep your eyes, ears and arms aligning.

Some will do things hoping not to hurt.
Others do things hoping to finish first.
You should do what has lifelong worth.

Unobserved, you become your routines -
Triggers, reactions, then you in between;
Check tendencies with an eye that's keen.

It can be a tone or an overall manner,
Bearing down like a banging hammer:
It is a loud call to raise your standard.

Pick up after yourself
As a matter of health,
And proof of wealth.

They may not know what is at stake,
And you may have no time to explain.
Better wording may just have to wait.

Right now it will be hard to know why
And you will waste your time if you try
So just find a way to mindfully comply.

When you need to move through busy places
Rather than imagining yourself in an oasis,
Discover your paradise in friendly faces.

You be the one to break the ice.
But instead of trying to be nice,
Just be intentional and concise.

Doing something that to you feels pure
Sheds habits of which you're not sure
Leaving only ones that easily endure.

One odd thing about intensity -
It can trigger spiritual density.
Why not retire this propensity?

What would that have you become?
It's best to know before you've begun
By studying more experienced ones.

Yes, there is a path that is perfect,
But a different way is also correct.
Figure out which one is most direct.

It's about more than just who can pay -
It's about if you like to work their way
And love hearing their voices every day.

Your anger is part of you for a reason:
To defend you against emotional treason
And arm you with your own inner legion.

Good conversation holds a loving sensation.
A great conversation births transformation.
So talk with more people who love creation.

They may or may not keep goal journals,
They may or may not have leaped hurdles,
They only need to honor your inner circle.

You may look back at the start of a trip,
But along the way, who you are shifts
Until today is the only thing that fits.

Ask people about what they know
And they will both tell and show
You new ways to think and grow.

Time is what you are letting them thieve
When you sit amongst but do not receive;
Their conversation starves you, so leave.

Do it for the sake of the adventure.
This way regardless, you'll treasure
The time all of you spent together.

It is good to have two different goals -
One to dream toward and one you can hold
To make it impossible to ever grow old.

Rearrange your life in better order
And there'll be more time to afford
To spend on those you truly adore.

You may have no trouble when you start
In doing something with less than heart,
But it will fall down, so take it apart.

CHAPTER 10

There is more of you you can call upon.
Go to the mirror, take time, look long.
It's there in your eyes: endless beyond.

Love is what makes you beautiful,
Love for yourself and for us all,
Love that is wholly irrefutable.

What helps you handle each change?
What in you has remained the same?
What you've found is where to stay.

At times the journey will feel mystical,
And at other times unbearably difficult.
That you just keep on going is critical.

Be right here where your power resides,
Drifting to nor fro despite rising tides,
Floating on the tranquility deep inside.

Emotional routines carve unmeant masks
That others copy to make their own cast.
How you choose to feel spreads and lasts.

Decide what you'd do despite the pain.
Decide what you'd let remain the same.
Decide what you're here now to change.

It's time to change your whole approach
Even if this calls for getting a new coach
Because habit on progress can encroach.

Starting is going to take a bit of trust,
Often not knowing why, just that you must
So let today be one wholehearted thrust.

Take not as genuine that which is guile:
A venomous snake also appears to smile.
Stand still and watch from here awhile.

Since you are doing it for deeper benefits,
You represent more than yourself with this
And must be mindful which partnerships fit.

Even after it has all been delivered,
You will still need to have considered
What your heart has already whispered.

Remain right here in the grip of the storm
Knowing deep inside you're safe and warm
Going through this in order to learn more.

Words meant purely in jest
May instead arrive to test
A relationship needing rest.

That coat was perfect for those storms
And now it is a bit tattered and worn;
Go on, take it off and wear it no more.

Acting on impulses will humble you when
You are asked to deliver the words again,
Forced to replay what you barely meant.

More people than is evident
Truly do appreciate silence;
Give it and see what you get.

What today holds is different for all,
Some will rise and others will fall;
You are blessed to heed your own call.

Draw from where you've been and improve;
Greatness follows no preexisting groove;
It follows those who make their move.

Hummingbirds fly fast, trees sway slow -
Most things in nature have a preset flow,
But you can change your pace as you go.

The basement is full - go upstairs.
Enjoy the view and the fresher air.
Everyone knows, but few go there.

If you don't get just what you expected,
You must see that it is you being tested
For what you yourself actually invested.

The same lesson is going to keep coming
Until you prove you're actually above it;
Learning to say no will be just as loving.

> Doubt lore, legends and such.
> Search until patterns turn up:
> It was by law and not by luck.

When mulling over which path to choose,
Make peace with what you intended to do;
Build upon what already comes from you.

And with whom you had most in common
Are those who misunderstand most often
That as you change, toughness softens.

Mend your fence and latch up your gate.
When the need comes it may be too late.
Boundaries are nothing to leave to fate.

> If that leads somewhere you dread,
> Why not do what you feel instead?
> Trust your heart over your head.

Once in a while, anger will be a useful tool.
Usually, it makes you appear to play the fool.
Either way, own the whole of it, as a rule.

Symptoms are rarely immediate: be aware.
If today's choice is made with more care,
It gives tomorrow so much less to bear.

Your purpose isn't to finish your tasks,
It's to be the one brave enough to ask
Why things need to be moving so fast.

How you send someone off after a defeat
Is a chance to perform a most noble feat:
To bow to their graciously given treat.

Lay your habits as carefully as bricks
Because once time gets each to stick,
They will withstand even direct hits.

You are the villain and they fight for glory
What if they deeply need this as their story?
Are you here to play out their flat allegory?

Let others choose what they will follow.
For you those options would feel hollow.
Which one makes your heart shout bravo?

There is a time to be wary of extremes,
Of mosts and bests, without in-betweens.
Neither glut nor starve: find your lean.

Yes, your mind can find you plenty.
There will just always be too many.
So if you can't do all, don't do any.

With or without training to speak of,
Develop a voice that makes you sit up,
That sounds like an instrument of love.

Until you ask, you will have no idea
Whose perspective can make life clear
As you try to find a way out from here.

"Almost there" means you're still measuring,
Thinking about what pleasure getting brings.
How much could you already be treasuring?

The reason they consider you a resource
Is that instead of making it about force,
You've wisely followed destiny's course.

The choices will keep getting more granular,
As you recognize expectation as the saboteur
Because you're simply no longer an amateur.

Reasons only seem deeply important. It's
Really how much feeling you afford them.
Your whys bloom as much you adore them.

Old superstitions might bully new ideas,
So to their warnings make it very clear:
You are doing something original here.

Let it out - you are allowed to complain
Because it can bring relief to the brain
Which is not meant for carrying disdain.

You always have the power to rewrite
Any part of this to create day from night
By opening to more inspiration and insight.

The greatest kept treasure is your time,
The treasure chest is your state of mind;
You are wealthy when both match in size.

What you love to hold, you sometimes drop.
When you do, it is just as important to stop
To see if you made a mess you need to mop.

Though you may be told this is impractical,
Imagine how you'd handle the unimaginable.
This will show you everything is manageable.

Become a student of history
And what they call a mystery
Will reveal itself swiftly.

Some people just prefer to oppose you -
It's something you'll have to go through
To discover all that you're supposed to.

Note how quickly you respond
To decide if you want to go on
Or say it's already too far gone.

Stubbornness forgets, or else never knows
That it's just an actor in your mind's show
With too few lines for anyone to take note.

Speak your mind, then hold your tongue.
What your words do is not easily undone;
Wisdom is verbally lost and silently won.

You grow apart, even without any strife
This is purely the ebb and flow of life
So don't let theories or tales run rife.

You wouldn'tve agreed if you'd known
And that is why you were only shown
Enough for this to begin to be grown.

Just as there are losing ways to fight,
There are even wrong ways to be right.
Let flow itself be your utmost delight.

Luck runs away from the idle.
Be just like a horse unbridled
Then it cannot escape or hide.

You are so close - you just need to stop.
Tear up your blueprints and entire plot.
The genius of chance is what you've got.

Life is locked and something holds the key?
Did you really come to solve some mystery?
Trust that you already know what is to be.

Your focus should be aimed at one thing
Or else you won't do enough of anything
To enjoy mastery's wonderful feeling.

Stop all that unconsciously apologizing,
Yielding time-space without recognizing
Mindless retreat keeps you from rising.

The finish is close. Dive for it. Leap!
To reach out and grab what you seek
Let everyone else choose to be meek.

Life is long. You have time. Calm down.
Wake up. Open your eyes. Look around.
Wiggle your toes deep into this ground.

You'll be served best by putting it down
It is what holds you here on the ground.
Let go and let the wind take you around.

As you keep at it every single day,
Heading into your own made up fray,
Time will surrender, bow down and pay.

You are surrounded on all sides by sages.
They will all reveal themselves in stages.
Be the pupil in each of today's exchanges.

Cherish your life in day-sized servings.
Weeks, months and years are all unworthy
Of focus because they're ever-diverging.

Those who "do" to please, crawl.
Do, just for the joy for it all.
Do - whether you fly or fall.

Thinking you know, you may deeply err.
Only through feeling can you get there.
Head will assume but heart rarely dares.

It's nothing but a word - a made-up name.
Without it, would you be acting the same?
With it, are you able to make some gain?

When you don't wish to be singled out
Those who point, criticize and shout
Remind you to take a different route.

Remind yourself that this is not a race
And that bandits also like a good chase;
No prize to win - just yourself to face.

Understand they are struggling through
And let compassion flow from within you
Without judging what they are up to.

If you do it that way, it won't be natural.
It's one thing to try and become masterful,
But more wondrous a journey to be gradual.

Choose the path that honors You,
Not where you are or what you do,
But how you are, and for now, who.

Keep on thinking about your alignment,
About what you need to be most vibrant,
About where to best await fate's timing.

Wrap your mind around this entire space.
Let no chance to learn more go to waste,
And share each as you put things in place.

Let comments fall like rain on your roof
Let them trickle all over or deluge you;
Let them come down, just never through.

Anything is bearable if you have a plan
So don't join the nay-sayers if you can;
Keep on climbing your own mountain.

Sometimes, for a time, you need to quit
So you can come back with a lighter grip
And by letting go, be true to your spirit.

Time to look at your current direction
Side-by-side with your life momentum
So you'll recognize useful connections.

The big problem with asking why
Is that this might not be the time;
Let understanding naturally arise.

You're wealthy when you're generous,
You're powerful when you're curious,
You're immortal when it's effortless.

All your doings should be more rigorous,
So nurture whatever keeps you vigorous
And map out all your inner wilderness.

When it doesn't seem to be about you,
But about what you can selflessly do,
You're rich because you contribute.

Forgiving transforms you, it truly does.
It rewrites your past in phrases of love
And ensures the future will rise above.

What you have is not who you are.
Where you go brings you near, not far:
Use your center as your guiding star.

Be willing. Be strong. Be rooted. Dig in.
When faced with chaos, perseverance wins.
Just deepen your stance and tuck your chin.

A slow start should always be preferred
Over a haste in which lines get blurred
To be fully present for all that occurs.

To keep getting what you currently get,
Yesterday's effort would be appropriate,
But today calls for an energetic reset.

To not go back, you must make a choice.
To go on, you'll need to use your voice.
To enjoy going, you'll need to rejoice.

For as long as your values align
Your happinesses should coincide
And you can be each other's guide.

The real problem is always perspective -
Never the details - just ask any detective:
Doubt all your hunches and be objective.

As you are bringing life to your dream,
It is vulnerable in this place between,
And needs you to leave all who demean.

If you get the chance, take fate's dare
Look it in the eye with an impish glare
At least for a time, chase it anywhere.

You're doing so much work, without a reward.
Whatever was coming, will multiply even more
As the result of sharing everything you adore.

You have traveled without expectations
And that has been good for contemplation;
Now it is time for conscious navigation.

Are you sure this is what you should do?
Yes? Then refuse to take on anything new
Until your schedule reflects your truth.

Don't rush to fill every awkward silence
To avoid disapproval or outright defiance:
These are not the times for compliance.

CHAPTER 11

Perhaps toward the very thing you feared
Is where your journey should be steered
Perhaps that is why the feeling is here.

This loving act may feel the opposite,
Because of the friends attached to it -
But you know that it is time to quit.

Something incredible is already waiting
So very nearby to where you are staying
Nothing you do will cause any delaying.

Going without is going to break you apart
Which then helps the transformation start
Which then reconnects you to your heart.

Not time for that - it is time for this
Regardless of whether you need to shift
Priorities rather than let them all mix.

Long-lasting is fine, but to what end?
What good is it to last but never bend?
Love stays vulnerable enough to mend.

Or you can find out by taking a detour;
It helps to go where you're not so sure
To recognize the one path that is yours.

Things haven't come together? What to do!
Tell it like it is, or dance around the truth?
Talk how you would prefer to be spoken to.

You keep standing in your own way
By hiding behind your own résumé.
Can you throw qualifications away?

It's those you didn't choose that matter
Those you can neither fire nor flatter -
Who are steps on your spiritual ladder.

It may feel new or seem like a leap,
Or like a hike that's a bit too steep,
But all this is is your time to reap.

It wasn't a mistake - it was necessary
To put a lesson in your bones to carry
So you can just know and not be wary.

When emotions rise and rage, face them.
You will be threatened but never taken,
Because you already decided to awaken.

You can figure this out - You are ready.
Aim with sharpened sight holding steady.
Target what's hiding behind what's petty.

Not what you are, but what you become
Is what to wonder, not how to be done;
Focus a bit more each day on having fun.

There's a time for nurture, a time to go;
Needing parenting is a thing to outgrow,
Shedding the seeking of anyone's say-so.

The trivialities you put in your own way
Are enough to lead your attention astray,
But not for long - so end this interplay.

This time allow the passage of some time
Before interrupting with logic and mind.
Step back and appreciate this grapevine.

Wanting to have that is a level of interest
That's good, but not better, and not best:
Wanting to give this outranks all the rest.

Timeless rewards go to undying faith:
You cannot know what wonders await
All thanks to your guarding the gate.

Conversation is such a life-giving act;
Half skill, half ritual best kept intact
Doing more than resuscitating facts.

Know you are living your life perfectly.
You have overcome what no one will see
To become this example of manifesting.

Expecting to be given a discount,
Rather than paying the full amount,
Is a gift that will come back around.

Your certainty makes you more effective.
It convinces them you have perspective,
And then renders your charisma electric.

It took foresight to avoid being misled.
And since you were brave enough to shed,
Your lightness helped you to move ahead.

Least important is where they come from;
Rather be sure you share the same tongue
In matters of positivity, work and love.

Perhaps the truest words you can bestow
Are ones that tell the unwelcome to go
For they do not help your garden grow.

Unkind thoughts must be thrown away
Lest over anything else they gain sway;
Let love and understanding own today.

Keep going because you are so very near
To another spot where the path is clear
Enough to prove that you belong here.

Do what energizes, not what drains.
No matter what, this advice remains.
What you enjoy is where you'll gain.

Look around and feel if you belong here,
Or if you're just settling for what's near:
Is the benefit of what's around you clear?

A breakthrough need not be announced
Because it becomes even more profound
Without interruptions from the mouth.

The best lessons are easy to understand
But hard to await patiently as they land
As lightly as a butterfly upon the hand.

And some connections need to be cut
To keep you from falling into a rut
Where it's hard to see what is what.

They want you to stop and go over there.
But all that going will get you nowhere.
Consider: does breathing go get its air?

Even though you feel caught in a loop,
You have actually already broken through
As proven by your new point of view.

Right now you indeed need to hurry up
Whether that means a push or a shove,
Finish it faster than you dreamed of.

The second you feel misaligned,
Or like an accomplice to a crime,
Give them no more of your time.

Visualize to properly use your brain
Because what you imagine, you ingrain
And what you think is how you train.

This is a wonderful journey. Do you see?
By deciding today will go just perfectly
Because joy is in choosing momentarily.

Don't seek more where you last lost.
Pay no more than what it already cost.
Consider this a border you've crossed.

To your relationships be most devout,
More than whatever you worried about
For to your bliss, they are the route.

Hopefully you can see you're much wiser,
Much more observant, yet far from a miser
In how you used this to open up wider.

Here is what will happen once you start:
Your head gets guidance from your heart
And everything will play its proper part.

Let it feel exactly as it does.
Go neither below it nor above.
Keep on flooding it with love.

The sun will shine again, even brighter.
Days are already getting a little lighter.
You can be the lover, retire the fighter.

If you understand that seasons change,
Why not embrace your own heart's range
And think none of your moods strange?

What you will gain will be worth the loss
Despite the deep emptiness it will cause:
To meet you, love has to first go across.

Your instincts are telling you correctly:
Yes, you should address it, and directly.
(Self-trust will soon feel elementary.)

Training your thoughts is not science
But pure persistence and self-reliance
And one great role model or alliance.

No, the teller told you a lie.
Those rules never did apply.
You were already right.

Too many things happened all at once,
But instead of reacting quite so much,
You need to let your presence show up.

Let them fret over what the future holds
Because even once it all seems unrolled,
It will refuse to be completely foretold.

Thank your thinking and now let it rest.
For what comes next it may be but a pest;
Heart is your home and mind but a guest.

Look at what's stewing in front of you.
Look at its intricacy as energetic proof:
Look at this as an exact opposite route.

An emotion is lightning without thunder,
But certainty gives it a deafening rumble:
Decide your weather, don't run for cover.

There are those who need you to react
To keep their inner world view intact:
Lovingly disarm all their petty traps.

If your mind plays with any doubt,
It is at the same time filtering out
The truth of what this is all about.

There is no need for defense or retreat
Once you decide to be unmoved by defeat
And choose to become impossible to beat.

You know you've closed a life chapter
When your belly holds healthy laughter
Over your unique happily-ever-after.

Kindness begins and ends with yourself,
For spiritual, mental and physical health.
This is the surest way for you to be well.

Spread allies out, around on each side.
You never know when you'll be surprised
And need someone else to turn your tide.

Imagine if instead of feeling needed
You were far more heard than heeded;
Would this have more or less appeal?

You won't even have to ask the question,
Won't even have a single need to mention
When you are living out your intention.

You should now be asserting yourself
Via firm handshake or wishing well;
Make an impression that is heartfelt.

The feeling of being embarrassed
Is a feeling to truly be cherished:
It's the way to carefree awareness.

You're not obligated to be what you were.
Look back to see your past as a vivid blur.
So decide anew based on what you prefer.

This body is your perfect vehicle
To journey all that's meaningful
And experience the unbelievable.

Forgive all those sellers of cheap things
Pressuring you to buy what they bring
Unaware you already have everything.

Know when to bring in other opinions,
Feel when to make your own decisions,
Sense when it is the time for division.

That was a bumpy and dangerous road.
You'd incur damage before you'd know.
Will you drive it again? Surely, no.

The part of you that wants to hide
Is sitting on what's deeper inside:
Dig just past it to your gold mine.

Break it down into daily tasks.
Then do each one and do it fast
And the worst part will be past.

Do you understand what they're about,
Before you follow them on their route?
Do they put more in or want more out?

The decision is not between that or this
But whether to consider a loss or a win
As the same, and just keep surrendering.

Which one's routine, which one's ritual?
Which one of your habits feels spiritual?
Which inspires you to be unconditional?

Be systematic - think about the steps.
Rearrange in your head what comes next.
Play until you are all done with stress.

Whether you remember how to or not,
  Be grateful to whatever you forgot,
    Because enough is as good as a lot.

You don't have to like their decision,
  But it's their life and their vision,
So you should move to avoid collision.

Expect the mind to deliver you doubt.
Give it some attention, just not clout:
Stop and listen if the warning shouts.

Create the boundaries for the space.
Cultivate what will then take place.
Clear all that should be thrown away.

Every day leave one unkind word unsaid,
And with better food for thought be fed,
And you'll be the owner of a clearer head.

Those who find problems, always find more
  Though you carry solutions to their door.
    Stop trying to win their inner civil war.

    Find someone you can use as a model
    In how to support and yet not coddle
    Those who are beginning to dawdle.

    Though it lets you feel some ease,
      Hold on to it, but only so briefly;
    It too, is little more than a story.

Today brightens or dims your tomorrows
Depending on if you sacrifice or borrow,
So one-by-one resolve all your quarrels.

Do, because there is no other chance.
Flow, because you are part of a dance.
Love, because life itself is a romance.

You recuperate by listening to feelings
Despite the cures that sound appealing
To go on your own journey of healing.

When you run out of hopeful things to say,
And feel certain you have now gone astray,
Intending to get there is actually the way.

When you need one, a teacher will appear
To grant lessons or to speak into your ear
What your soul has been waiting to hear.

You are not here to rebuild or fix -
You are not here for any bit of this.
You are here to create your Oasis.

Signs simply wait to be read.
You're speeding by one again.
Rely on the eyes of a friend.

That chapter has long since ended;
Parts of it have already fermented.
Take fresh ones that are presented.

You can think you understand what's going on,
But you're better off assuming you're wrong;
What you need to do is just continue along.

How much do you identify with your name?
As for your stories, are you doing the same?
Do these even begin to describe your range?

You have this knowing in your bones,
That good ones have colorful tones -
So mix some and enjoy others alone.

Which part of you will you let choose -
The one that usually gets you to refuse,
Or the one that always finds your muse?

However long it takes, so be it,
For you to open up and free it,
For you to let the world see it.

They don't have to have what you need -
You have to be able to quickly perceive
To know if they do, then stay or leave.

Enough thought about what you'll begin!
The day to imagine's the day you are in.
It is the proven habit that's the win.

CHAPTER 12

Become entire
As air is to fire:
Give up desire.

How you see the exact same thing
Determines how every day begins,
So make a ritual of perceiving.

What you make will be greater than its parts
If you give it the best, earliest, farthest start;
All you'll ever need are momentum and heart.

You learn something when you procrastinate -
Time can be commanded to serve you in haste.
Can you leverage this truth without being late?

Giving something a chance, doesn't guarantee
Everything will fall into place uneventfully.
Yet whatever you decide, say it respectfully.

Clean your space until it feels spacious,
Not so you can appear neat or gracious,
But so you can find your work's basis.

You will need something to go between
So that everything goes forward easily;
What could help everyone else agree?

When you find yourself on guard
Over tasks that feel overly large,
It comes time for you to recharge.

Where there is nervousness there is what?
What can those doubts help you dream of?
When is it time to be nervous about love?

Should you go get it or wait for it to come?
Either way, first see to it that this is done:
Make room precisely where there is none.

It is alright to change your mind.
Decisive people do it all the time
Based on the new things they find.

The more time you spend trying to explain,
The more questions will come just the same.
Work on your masterpiece - not on its name.

Silence is difficult for the maladjusted
By whom you find yourself interrupted.
Who cannot be quiet cannot be trusted.

Require positivity of yourself. Insist.
Invites to fume or fuss or feud, resist.
Speak brightly as light piercing mist.

We all possess the same powers -
We all own the same 24 hours;
We all build tombs or towers.

Whether intentional or just by accident,
If it keeps you from your accomplishment
Then it is the opposite of an advocate.

Even if perfection is your personal goal,
They don't care if it's half-done or whole;
They only seek some time with your soul.

Things that are solid hold their ground
And whatever tied to, they'll pull down;
Just figure out what needs to be bound.

How long will it take to build?
Who all has the required skills?
What vision will this fulfill?

Smile about where you find yourself now.
Give all due credit to your own know-how
With one great big, self-celebrating bow.

Regardless of meeting your own goal,
By making your learned lessons known
You'll make everyone who hears whole.

Stepping outside everyone else's rules,
Your sincerest and clearest way, choose.
Decide, using your own highest values.

You block yourself from knowing what's coming
By thinking you need just a little more cunning.
You'll know it all when you find it all stunning.

==Take longer breaks between each action==
To review what brings you satisfaction
And revisit what causes which reaction.

Do not fall for it - you are being set up
To return to what you were once made of;
Stay within the light of your self-love.

Lead your way by being perfectly clear
Because whether or not they even hear,
This is how the heart learns to steer.

There is a great benefit to noise -
It challenges you to practice poise.
When life is louder than your voice.

Who can say what happens next?
Does uncertainty call for stress?
The unknown knows what's best.

==Sometimes we can use the past as an excuse.==
Other times it can be put to very good use.
Those who rewrite yours count as fools.

Or else nothing needs to change -
Because things that stay the same
Help you sharpen your aim.

Is it better to have well-sharpened wit
Or just an awareness of when to give in?
Sometimes the one who loses truly wins.

Keep your space clean and keep it clear
So that confusion has nowhere to appear
And inspiration knows it's welcome here.

The day's an hourglass filled with sand;
Each soul you meet a grain yet so grand.
Take every chance to extend a kind hand.

Bypass roads that run shrouded in dark,
That twist round corners or seem stark.
Head toward the light, guided by heart.

Stubbornness only needs one false step
For others to heckle under their breath;
Reasonability works much better instead.

For decisions like this, talk to someone
Who had to get something like this done.
Minds can work better as two than as one.

What is it that you're waiting to hear?
You have proof your thinking is clear
And the feeling that you're very near.

The future you dream of, is it external?
If so, it is but the smallest of a kernel
Of a harvest that is already internal.

There is most certainly a price to pay:
What you were in exchange for this way;
Every tomorrow in exchange for this day.

Set out with more than a running start
To give even more support to your heart
As it does what makes you stand apart.

When you do not need even one more thing,
That is when you can acutally begin to bring
Gifts to all - whether they criticize or cling.

What draws a crowd tends to hide behind noise.
Find yourself groups that pause for every voice,
Because hearing is actually your bravest choice.

Safeguard by investing in your own idea,
Something that uses your current career
To look where your vision is most clear.

Protect your nest but know when to stop,
So you do not end up hatching some plot
That doesn't build upon what you've got.

Climb the higher ground toward your goal
By sacrificing today what's comfortable.
Self-discipline is worth itself in gold.

The habit of how you talk to someone
Certainly cannot overnight be undone,
So try things day by day - one by one.

Here is one you simply must try:
Just journey without asking why
And where the road ends - fly.

Is it a thankless task or mindful work?
Either - wherever your focus goes most.
So take the time to train that to turn.

When given the words you prefer to hear,
Treat your ears as eyes that keenly peer
Past them to what quickly draws near.

Does kindness strive to dominate?
Does fairness move to manipulate?
Does simplicity try to complicate?

Look at what is standing right there.
Examine it all with painstaking care.
What can you use - how and where?

What is given as a gift is meant for you
Whether or not you can put it to good use
It is a chance to exercise your gratitude.

Take the time to ask about their stories,
About their hardships and their glories,
To learn how they outworked worries.

Offer a question instead of a defense
Whenever asked to explain your intent;
Where you're going - not where you went.

The heart doesn't have nearsightedness.
When you use it to see you'll find this,
That they haven't found their way yet.

Yes indeed - they gave you an ultimatum.
Know it's nothing more than a statement
Reminding you it's time to stop waiting.

Though the proposal might sound absurd,
==Stay mindful of your every chosen word==:
How you respond is what gets overheard.

See questions and ideas as kinds of fuel,
Or as only-briefly sharp-enough tools
You know when and how long to use.

Pack light. Set out. Just start traveling.
Staying put, things will start unraveling.
What lies ahead is nothing short of dazzling.

Do your part of the work,
And if your helpers shirk,
Let this teach, not hurt.

The planning is done. It is time to do.
Enough thinking. That time is through.
Begin the routine and begin with you.

Acknowledging everyone you meet today
Is like lighting torches along the way
Just by having something warm to say.

Refuse to judge it, and it will move on.
Stay where you are. Be consciously calm.
You be the landmark that you base upon.

Limiting words create limiting beliefs.
Lighter words make lightness increase.
Words are for you to catch and release.

As long as you keep going back to the start,
You'll keep making it harder for your heart
To express itself and take your story apart.

Focus is waiting for your sacrifice,
Not to ensure things turn out right,
But to re-aim with sharpened sight.

If you dislike the term procrastinating,
Then think of it as an internal debating
Only won through attempts, not waiting.

The hardest decisions you have to make
Are pointing out which excuses are fake
And letting them go for your own sake.

Don't bother deciding who you'll become.
Think about how much you want to have fun
And give this your life's days, one by one.

In case you were seeking an outside verdict,
No one ever needed your need to be certain:
You are most beautiful when you're imperfect.

The reason you worried about it at all
Is that your vision was still too small;
On other dreamers, it is time to call.

Some search for themselves by using you.
While yet an honor, it has nothing to do
With your purpose or what you're up to.

Imagine your most wonderful version,
The one boldly going on that excursion;
You're already becoming that person.

Being angry enough to fight
Doesn't make you or it right;
Your grip on life is too tight.

Channel your passion.
Take immediate action.
Note: Put off satisfaction.

Is this the time and place to share?
Are you surrounded by those who care?
By people already awake and aware?

It's going to be a mistake if you do assume
Things will all work themselves out soon:
Consciously create your breathing room.

You will find stillness outlasts skill.
Hiking mindfully beats dashing uphill,
And serenity is a better ally than will.

Open up a little bit more of your attention
To take in all the beauty in every direction
And feel how it immediately cures tension.

Go over each thing you do, thoroughly,
And check that it is still unswervingly
Taking you to where you want to be.

If it were otherwise it wouldn't be true
So get some sleep, wake up and continue
And you will soon enough have your proof.

It's alright to find yourself in a mess.
It's alright to walk in a fog of stress.
It's alright to not return here again.

Too much certainty leads to confusion;
You have to work on constant evolution
To become a fountain of new solutions.

Keep yourself organized because of this:
Whatever response will need to be quick,
And you must know where everything is.

Training is the reason you act this way.
The grooves were cut deep so you'd stay.
Escape options? You have a whole array.

Schedule time to just walk away,
To give your mind space to stray
And keep predictability at bay.

Let your heartbeat be your guide today:
It races when there is something to say
And slows when life is perfectly okay.

You are comfortable here for a reason:
You know how to dress for this season;
But your wardrobe is becoming uneven.

Consider each word an energetic marker:
When words seem to be getting harsher,
Perhaps you need an earlier departure.

Anger is a defense. Now end your war.
You do not need to fight against or for
What was only ever meant to be a door.

Whether or not they show their support,
No diversion to which you could resort
Would be worth it, for time is short.

What does succeeding have to do with it?
Put your focus solely on the movement.
All lose who think in terms of some win.

Everyone is looking out for you
Interacting to help you improve
Through everything that they do.

Bad examples can provide the best advice
Needing to neither be packaged nor nice.
Listen to every life for the lessons inside.

Once you're creating, it's less about you
And more about letting it pass through -
The messages being sent from your muse.

Must it sound the way they say it should
To make a difference or to even be good?
Are you here to be, or to be understood?

It is time to embrace You and share.
Trust it and lay your own soul bare.
You are so perfectly incredibly rare.

The words themselves are nearly useless.
How they're delivered is the truest test.
Forgo what's said to hear what's meant.

First you got to enjoy feeling inspired,
After that, your presence was required.
Now, you need genuine rest when tired.

Before you hear the howling of the wind
Is when your stormproofing must begin;
It is the time to build things, not listen.

CHAPTER 13

Wisdom will not come from what others say -
Mistakes make experience, it's the only way;
Failing is nothing more than a price to pay.

It's best to find others who are also seeking,
Because when people on a quest are meeting
They all stop starting and start completing.

What now offers you feelings of stress
Is actually a simple point-of-view test
In both understanding and forgiveness.

Tomorrow's decisions are easier today,
If you can see far enough down the way
Or ask those who went but didn't stay.

All you can do is what you can do.
As for the rest, it is not up to you,
So decide what you want to be true.

If you can look past each circumstance,
And past every opportunity to advance,
You'll see your genuine, actual chance.

It's not enough to know - you need tools
To shape things into a form you can use;
How else do you build what you choose?

As soon as you're no longer chasing,
And have had enough of past-erasing,
You and true peace will be embracing.

Consider this your sign to move on,
A warning you've been here too long
And proof you should already be gone.

Catch things before they become an issue
Just as your organs faithfully do for you;
Clear inner pathways hold clearer truths.

It will take them a while to understand
So rather than leading them by the hand,
Prove by passion that it will be grand.

It can feel right - chasing enemies down
Until you catch up and turn them around
And see it's you yourself you have found.

You can live as perfectly as you like,
And remain unfulfilled on the inside,
So seek to grow gratitude, not pride.

It's as easy to slip into another realm
As it is to dive into what you've felt:
You'll go farther than words can tell.

Appreciate every one of your cravings:
How they can instigate some misbehaving,
Yet thanklessly handle daily lifesaving.

==Take it gradually, using what you've got==
==Otherwise you'll put yourself in a spot;==
==This way it's easier to unravel the knot.==

Doing a thing to get a thing is suspect.
Doing a thing to be that thing is correct.
Doing must be kept in constant check.

You may still think you need to strive
To make sure your vision stays alive:
==Honest love is all it needs to thrive.==

It's easiest once it fits some kind of picture
To help figure out what goes where quicker
And you can know if you end up the victor.

There is no point in forever responding.
To hear yourself should get you yawning.
You're the sun - it is time for dawning.

It's good to have a tendency to jest,
But not if it's just a way to deflect
From admitting your preciousness.

When do you feel perfectly safe?
Is it at the very end of your day?
Or the moment it gets underway?

Learning has helped you feel qualified,
For everything except what waits inside;
For this you need to trust and confide.

They are only doing what you chose to see
Demonstrated outside of you - externally -
Because you want to look at this thoroughly.

Where others stopped is not far enough;
Because what they considered too rough
Is just where you must drop some stuff.

The power of your internal connections
Creates these outside-world reflections
So look around you in all directions.

From great guidance to bad examples,
Wisdom in every form you can handle
Is lighting your path's 10,000 candles.

You sit in the theater of the uncertain
Ready and able to pull back the curtain
Rest assured, the play will be worth it.

You need to be working on your craft,
Because all you have already amassed
Points to the future - but is the past.

Minding the details is important,
But only once you establish order,
So first get the overall sorted.

When suffering is what you've been granted,
There's no point wishing to feel enchanted:
You'll have to bloom where you are planted.

Be at peace with disappointing others.
Wiser to beware their fog of druthers,
Smoke that blinds before it smothers.

Smile at challengers - right in the face.
Via clever surprise, leap and give chase.
Via wit and will, put all in their place.

The error of judging them is behind you,
Mastering forgiveness and starting anew.
This time around, let opinions be few.

Put more focus on the how than the what
And more time with the if than the but;
It is the sharpening that makes the cut.

With many ways in but one way out,
You may be wisest to go on without
Until you know what this is about.

Once you feel it, it will be known
Before that, it's hard to be shown.
Only what you are will you own.

Your hard work can become its own addiction
That is only satisfied when you feel friction:
Can gracefulness become your life mission?

End your search for the right question
And let the answers get your attention
By walking away from comprehension.

Keep on. Forward! Ignore those voices,
The ones that offer distracting choices.
Momentum will drown out side noises.

The way forward is the one most gentle
That will use your subconscious mental,
As you train it with some fundamentals.

You have one job - to keep progressing,
Not to be measuring or second-guessing,
Or even spending your time confessing.

Temper prowls with mouth open wide,
To devour whoever will not move aside
And take the flow of events in stride.

Whatever stays stable will resist change
And this applies the same to your brain,
So spend more time with the unexplained.

What if there's no training left to work toward?
What if you throw all those steps out the door?
What if you're already here - needing no more?

You really need to give yourself time
For everything to come together inside
Before you can take all this in stride.

It may not matter as much as you think,
Though this may feel as if it's a brink;
It really is as fleeting as one blink.

What makes you healthy is unique to you.
Eat nothing but what your senses approve,
And pay attention the whole way through.

It may not match with your perspective,
But instead of playing detail-detective,
Why not take the time to be reflective?

Though it feels like pointless abuse,
What feels hardest to put to good use
Is a box holding transformative truth.

Infatuation with dates, facts and names
Is one form of love but is not the same
As daring to touch and risking the pain.

Be steady in who you see yourself to be
And yet willing to change into anything
That your vision tells you is necessary.

So long as you have nothing to prove,
And know exactly what you are up to,
You can put everything to good use.

If you make your hands work too hard,
They'll start to put up their own guard
Against instead of for assistance's arm.

The way through this, or any struggle
Is to deeply know all of your numbers
So nothing is left to doubt or wonder.

This is not done, but you need to get going,
Toward people who you need to be showing
So this gets more nourishment for growing.

The same way the sun daily sets,
Get away and create time to rest.
This is the way to be your best.

Don't focus on the path in the heat;
Focus instead on how your own feet
Are holding up and what they need.

To find the way to your heart's desire
Look at your list of priorities entire
And rearrange your day as it requires.

There's a limit to the number of tasks
That can fit inside your life's baskets
What should they hold is what to ask.

Which of your talents has most impact?
Which does more than keep you intact?
To which one do you keep coming back?

If you have to manage it to that degree,
Then maybe it's best to just let it be -
You can't be tending that constantly.

There's nothing to buy, nor to believe,
No one to follow, nor for you to lead -
Only roles to shed, here and now to be.

This way that you are treating yourself,
Is this how you would treat anyone else?
Do you believe kindness creates health?

You are wise to turn from some journeys,
To roll up those maps and sound retreat,
When just pressing on is just unhealthy.

Move your dream forward one step today.
Come up with some half hour-long foray.
Confidence grows from little hoorays.

Decide to get from it just what you need
And the time will pass more easily indeed;
Perspective is the voice you should heed.

Have nothing to do with it;
Being given is the opposite
Of getting via will and grit.

Today's hard, but keep the long view.
Look far down the road for the truth
Today's journey brings you closer to.

Some place their attention on the pain,
While others look past that to the gain;
To your soul, you are you just the same.

Doesn't it keep you in this spot?
Doesn't it ask of you quite a lot?
What would happen if you forgot?

Whether you're inclined to cheer aloud,
You should take one moment to be proud
Of everything your vision has endowed.

You embody what is precious about life,
So drop here now, any remnant of strife.
In this, your enlightenment has arrived.

Difficulty is neither friend nor enemy,
But that from which you choose to see
Each violent wave or one peaceful sea.

It's the result of each and every habit;
The routine is what reaches to grab it.
The craving did not create the pattern.

Regardless of intention, the effect was what?
To deliver you a solution or leave you stuck?
You need better alliances - not better luck.

And now get ready to outdo yourself -
Precedents are there to surpass or else
You risk sitting your power on a shelf.

What it leads you to, through, and from
Are new ways to grow in truth and love,
And challenge what used to be enough.

Your vision is stuck behind your beliefs.
Other people can provide you with relief,
Offering to be your extra hands and feet.

Whether you succeed on a global scale,
 Or thank the lessons of a genuine fail,
A journey's only worth what it entails.

   This avalanche of assignments
   Might make others feel tense -
   But let it awaken deeper sense.

Drop should-haves, maybes and oughts;
Lead your mind toward its best thoughts.
Show it what body and soul have brought.

  What thought could bring you relief?
  Why not think this rather than seek?
  As you do, is there any goal to meet?

You succeed alongside who you befriend;
Time is the money you must daily spend
Funding those on whom you will depend.

Until the lesson feels like your own skin,
And likewise protects what's vital within,
You may have to do this again and again.

There are two ways to go about this:
Wait until you have to make a shift,
Or be mindfully proactive about it.

Recognizing is very different from regret:
Recognizing creates a whole new mindset.
Recognizing the past helps what's not yet.

Ignore what's happening. Schedule progress
Because you get to decide what comes next.
Dedicating time is in and of itself, success.

In your recipe, they would be the spice:
Some pungent, riling; others mild, nice.
Flavoring is just that - not core advice.

Hurdle the pit of overthinking
Wherein effort ends up sinking;
Be as certain as your blinking.

Take some time to reestablish order,
To review and redefine your borders,
To remind yourself you are important.

Do you desire to be seen or to observe?
Are you looking to receive or to serve?
Must something be given in return?

Those who benefit - do you know how?
Past what they say, does proof abound?
If so, great - if not, get yourself out.

Regardless of you feeling inconsistent,
It is time for you to be an instrument.
There is something you now represent.

This is the time to gather up speed and try
Before the opening is no longer this wide.
Swiftness is necessary at this exact time.

Healing arrives hand-in-hand with calm
To listen to whatever they called "wrong"
And through tenderness keep you strong.

Advice is never as good as the giver:
Look within the one who delivers
For living wisdom that shimmers.

If there are two roles that need filling,
Take the one that makes you more willing,
Not the one that others say is thrilling.

This may feel like a good time to plan
Rather than finish the mission at hand;
But focus and fulfill as only you can.

If you could see more of what others see,
You would be energized with an urgency
To hurry up and make what you believe.

CHAPTER 14

You are far from having reached your peak
Because what goes with being this unique
Is that you light the lanterns others need.

Even the worst parts can be entertaining
When you consider how silly is straining,
Like watering flowers when it's raining.

This is all you need: make the decision.
Don't be too attached to fine precision.
Trust the accuracy of your inner vision.

Just listen whether they rant or rave.
Develop your own new way to behave,
One that considers acceptance brave.

That place where thoughts like to dwell
Is simply their former hermit crab shell;
Out in the open is where you'll do well.

Darkness is good for narrowing your sight
So you can undeniably recognize the light
From what seemed dim. Now how bright!

You have forgotten how difficult it was
When you were first doing what you love
Now you easily know what to get rid of.

Listen closely or long enough to hear it:
That warning not to go anywhere near it
Because you cannot stop, start or steer it.

Whether or not you've finished your plan,
Surprises will meet you where you stand;
So handle them with heart, not with hand.

You were loving to give of your time.
Now lovingly say, "The rest is mine,"
Out of respect for your peace of mind.

You've outgrown fitting in with anyone,
Heedlessly brilliant as the noonday sun.
Just being yourself you warm everyone.

Let them tell you it's unbelievable
As your knowing defies the physical
And creates completely new material.

Between passion and patience, pick the one
That's best today for getting the job done,
Or else will let you have the most fun.

Make Levity and Lightness your friends.
A life lived with laughter knows no end;
Its tales retold rebirth laughter again.

Organize tomorrow today -
Next week, the same way;
Unschedule all disarray.

Doing the things you are supposed to do
Is the shortest path to reach your truth,
But it will still have its surprises, too.

So long as you know your dependencies,
One by one, you can deal with tendencies
To deny, deflect, confront or please.

You're naturally and constantly training
Everyone around you to avoid complaining
So the goodness becomes self-sustaining.

A rut is good, both to measure how deep
A thought can dig a hole and go to sleep,
And how high to escape you have to leap.

Plant your stake here in the ground.
Whether you rest, climb on or hike down,
Mark it and look all the way around.

Growing into a sense of self-worth is
Like knowing what to do with thirst:
Best to find where water flows first.

It's not about getting more things done.
It's about making time between each one
To notice what each helps you become.

Go find that place between open and wild
Where you have the potential of a child,
An imagination that's anything but mild.

More than ever, you need organization
To tuck away any and all complication
As you devote time to deep relaxation.

What you heard, you can't just un-hear,
But the words cease to reach your ear
When you start to be absolutely clear.

When will you allow yourself to be You?
Stop saying you don't know what to do!
You know it all, including the truth.

> They don't know:
> You must go slow
> So you can grow.

But this time they see more than you can,
The entire horizon and not just the land.
Beside them for awhile is where to stand.

> If they prefer to talk,
> They're already caught:
> You hurry up and walk.

It comes from where you least expect -
The guidance you will be needing next,
So be open and have both ears prepped.

You will feel like you're being left behind,
But that is not what should be on your mind:
You are at work on becoming one of a kind.

You are still doing more than you might
Were something else to hold you alight.
Do a bit less. It will all be just right.

Some spend a lifetime waiting for them
Only to realize right near the very end,
Leaving would've led to better friends.

Leave preferences aside and get moving on,
On toward your own daily innermost dawn,
On toward the whispers from your beyond.

Let go of repeating the same old cycle again:
Let the wanting-working-getting loop end -
Let you and what you enjoy become friends.

Whenever you run straight into a block,
Some surface of sheer, impassable rock,
There's an entrance to find and unlock.

Grace beats effort so, work on your flow.
Shift from doing only what you can show.
Become the spirit that harmony bestows.

What are the words you unthinkingly use
When trying to push yourself to choose?
Which are the words it is time to lose?

Some prefer to take it all in at once.
This is a habit that is rarely undone,
So just tend to your own digestion.

Body needs mind as mind needs heart.
You are less useful without every part,
Like canvas by itself trying to be art.

Help doesn't need to be your last resort.
This time, it'll be wisest to stop short.
Stay here and wait for a bit of support.

As you grow the faith to rise up and out,
You also outgrow status, pomp and clout;
Something amazing is starting to sprout.

Rise in relation to where you have been.
That was fine then, but not once again.
It is never too late or soon to begin.

Without needing to be the judge or the jury,
Without absorbing the passion, pain or fury,
Give everyone the right to their own story.

Feel back to all those bound-up thoughts.
Most were simply what you'd been taught.
To feel today, cut all those frayed knots.

You never know who knows who,
So be mindful what you're up to.
Only share what you know is true.

Attitudes reflect you the same as clothes:
Too big or small and people will suppose
You don't check yourself from top to toes.

Face up to the changes and adapt to them.
You're better now than you were back then.
So keep this in mind and head in again.

Look at what you are doing to yourself
To see whether it benefits your health
Or just echoes what someone else felt.

Keep on creating - no matter what comes,
Don't try wondering when you'll be done
Just focus on effort mixed in with fun.

Some circular stories never go away,
They just turn slower every new day
Until they are a statue of yesterday.

You can be comfortable you chose right,
And at very least you prevented a might
From ruining your well-deserved delight.

People speak the language they are taught
So in confusing phrases, don't get caught;
Keep on translating only what you ought.

Mistakes are the soul of transformation,
Teaching you focus through tribulation:
Less judgment and more contemplation.

Whatever unravels you again and again
Is just asking life's toughest question:
Whatever you want, can you first lend?

Sift their words for pebbles and chaff,
Ideas that do not keep you on track or
Untested advice that may set you back.

Pick any friendship to take measurement
Of how much is heard, how much is said.
If there's an even mix it is far from dead.

A spoken word has a creative vibration
That can create and spread inspiration,
So listen to what has sound foundation.

Whether a short or long-term friend,
They can help round this next bend
Like no other guide you have can.

Above all, are you enjoying yourself?
Does this thing improve your health?
You'll only treasure how you felt.

Pain is allowed. Let it flow right by.
Bear witness with a compassionate eye,
Remembering that trust makes it subside.

Your balance has benefitted just as much
From all the habits you never picked up,
As the ones you've never tried to hush.

The differences will, at first, seem slight:
One's a gentle landing, one a constant rise.
Why not choose to soar rather than glide?

There are so many moving parts.
Nonetheless, you have to start.
Details do not faze your heart.

Since you know you can go anywhere,
Get yourself up and fully out of there,
Up to where you can take in fresh air.

You feel you were clear, yet still ignored -
And of this cycle you've grown truly bored:
Your levels of directness are what to explore.

Listen to what is being offered -
Is it being said to sound proper?
Is it from a real doer or a talker?

Be flexible and open to their suggestion
Because regardless of a hidden intention
Every new idea raises a useful question.

What was unwanted is the gift,
For all that what's unwanted shifts,
Forcing expectation to give in.

If you are so lucky as to find laughter,
Better everything will come right after
Since you'll already have what matters.

If you stay in this funk, you get to see
That those patterns have no originality
And that you need new ones in actuality.

They've given their trust; you owe them
More than promising words and sentiment
You must now deliver something definite.

Growth is set to happen no matter what.
You just have to be willing to shed stuff
And sprout new powers on your way up.

It's fitting that you don't get to see the rest,
Because that would make this like some test;
This goes beyond every good, better and best.

It can take some time to change direction -
To see where you are and make a correction,
So be patient as you do some introspection.

Don't let their wording steer you wrong;
You're where you wanted to be all along.
You'll never need to argue to be strong.

You won't get to decide what goes,
But by believing what you know
Loss becomes a part of flow.

You don't have to know ahead of time,
But once you do, it will feel sublime
And you'll write your own next line.

If they tell you you have to choose,
Do they also have something to lose?
Why can you not be left to peruse?

Those who want better will try to do so;
Don't be a judge of what you don't know.
Many who struggle try hard not to show.

It is absolutely all about your attitude:
Great health comes from a great mood,
So let laughter spill into every room.

Are you shying away from the center?
Let this be your momentary mentor:
We go where we are ready to enter.

There's little you do someone else can't.
It's how you do it that forever enchants:
Everyone here loves to watch you dance.

Who last told you what you ought to do?
Don't let one bit of it stick to your shoe
Trailblazing the wilderness you choose.

"Stop changing your mind. Stay the same."
This advice is how to turn creativity plain.
Innovation lets itself be considered insane.

The moment you rise is when to begin.
Instead of expecting this chance again
Use today to grant the wishes within.

The answer does not need to come to you,
Rather it is you who will come to truth
By daily doing what it is that you do.

Now more than ever aim your focus
Away from patterns you want broken
And onto the path you have chosen.

You no longer have time for conversations
That involve useless, unkind speculation.
Your time belongs to your re-education.

Surprises do not change who you are -
They poke fun at the "easy" and "hard"
And remind you adaptability goes far.

Some say that love is a fiery emotion,
As intoxicating as some magic potion.
No. You are a wave. Love is the ocean.

If some result is in the back of your mind,
Your motivation will eventually unwind;
Loving your process should be your why.

Decide to do your best.
This must be stressed:
Yes - regardless - yes!

When you are told not to worry
By those who may be in a hurry,
It's because their view is blurry.

Building up from the ground is unwise.
Up from foundations do buildings rise,
So location is as important as supplies.

The way you need to be thinking right now
Is a way that no one has taught you how -
A way that begins the moment you allow.

When there are too many new things to do,
Is precisely when you need to kindly refuse
To be pushed, pulled or in any way moved.

The vast unknown is no cause for alarm;
Nothing out there can do you any harm;
Like a trained bird, call it to your arm.

Perhaps difficult, but you must sit still
To meet your own restless ambition's will
And ask it which cup it's trying to fill.

Going forward takes more than spending,
It takes humility and true heart rending.
Even in life, the soul can be ascending.

CHAPTER 15

Some old friends will just fade from view
As you continue heading somewhere new;
Those who come along are a priceless few.

You do not need to be any smarter
Nor do you need to work any harder,
You just need to walk a bit farther.

Your instinct is rarely wrong -
Though proof might take long.
But depend on it. It is strong.

Helping is going to be your universal key
To get started and done with everything:
So first of all, go give what others need.

It's as useful to go where it's easy
As it is where you might feel queasy:
We learn whether or not it's appealing.

Everyone may say, but you won't hear or
See it until you can look in the mirror
Loving yourself day-by-day ever-dearer.

Judging the steps you have taken
As the right ones or as mistaken
Is trying to sleep - not awaken.

Observe you yourself listening to this,
That so simply put - everything exists,
Including there being no need to get it.

Do not obsess about it - just calm down.
Something inside you knows the way out.
You will never need to think about how.

Accept that they ignored what you said.
Accept that they must clean their mess.
Accept that you have a garden to tend.

Keep everything in order and in tune
Because health is your greatest boon,
Making you rich right now, not soon.

It is time to change your tactics -
Yes, perhaps try something drastic,
Try anything except staying static.

Whether you get help or do it all alone,
Put in the work to make this your home.
As much as you choose will be your own.

Make sure that everything is connected,
Even what is hardest to get redirected;
Join them yet also keep them protected.

You might let them dispute your worth,
But let them know what you value first
To bring the whole thing down to earth.

Learn all of it for yourself
So that even if darkness fell
You could generate new wealth.

If it's going on like this, unresolved,
You have to get new people involved,
To show the old ones how to evolve.

Time is not something you can earn,
Nor can you make time pass or burn;
So time should not be your concern.

Give yourself completely over
To wanting to get even closer
To what brings more exposure.

Some of your routines, never ever lose -
Other ones it is time to pick and choose.
Some pretend to go, but it's just a ruse.

You're going to be relearning as you go,
Because of the gradual way life unrolls:
You do and do and then deeply know.

Sometimes it's best to plow on through
Despite the reasons they're giving you;
If given as an excuse, it's rarely true.

Of all the things you love to do,
Those that will most uplift you
Fill others with that feeling too.

Was that last journey too hard to repeat?
Would you rather find a comfortable seat?
Or do you feel restlessness in your feet?

If it's about tasks, you'll never be done.
If it's about levels, they'll never be won.
If it's about you, it will be forever fun.

Old or new stories about enemies and allies
Are not even tales - they're all genuine lies,
Strange words that love does not recognize.

You are not here to fulfill their goals
Nor are you here to do as you're told;
You are here to be imperfect yet bold.

Get ready, amazing connections are coming,
Ones that will have all your senses buzzing,
Moving faster than they have been running.

If you don't like the way it sounds,
Perhaps they overstepped their bounds.
Do they stand on justifiable ground?

Honesty. Mislead for no one.
Untruths shrivel in the sun;
Clarity blooms for everyone.

Like a shark who picks two fish to hunt,
Chasing two things, you only catch one:
You shouldn't be doing so much at once.

Open your arms. The world will come.
It wants to respond with so much love
And meet you in your pursuit of fun.

It is a wise practice to plan far in advance
To make time to take more than one chance
And still accept life's invitation to dance.

That may be exactly the way not to go -
The one where the riverbanks overflow;
Turn before your steps reach tomorrow.

So many things don't need doing,
So many facts don't need proving;
So much feeling goes into choosing.

Be polite with your faults - be polite.
No "How long until they turn right?"
Realize they obey only loving insight.

Resist their current before you get caught.
Spend more of your time where you ought,
Outside the flow of your river of thoughts.

Take this moment as your gift -
Not to be opened then dismissed
But to truly use what's within.

Forget about proving it -
But be all about doing it
By just truly choosing it.

Your arrival has been especially important
To so many voices that have lain dormant,
Awaiting you, to get beautifully recorded.

It's fine to let excitement come.
You deserve the feeling. It's fun.
But there's still work to be done.

Faithfully follow your plan for the day,
But of course be open to destiny's sway.
If asked to, unquestioningly give way.

You needed it, but now complain no more.
It helped you sweep your feelings' floor
In preparation for new blessings galore.

Enough of trying to meet their demands
That always use the work of your hands;
Root your two feet. In stillness stand.

Is this what you actually believe?
Have you lived it or merely seen?
What within you does this please?

There is more to you than you could know.
This how you can ignore what today shows.
This is why what matters now is your flow.

   Wake from daydreaming. Get to work.
   Put your schedule and structure first;
   Digging a well takes more than thirst.

Don't respond to every knock at your door
Or else distraction will demand even more
And invite confusion to make visits galore.

   The reasons are rarely as loud as news,
   But latest events are not of much use.
   Stick with clear thoughts as your tools.

   A few key things you need to increase:
   More water, rest and nutrients to eat
   For the clarity you're going to need.

   Hear your default inner monologue.
   Is it describing a journey or a slog?
   Exactly who is bringing who along?

If you're conflicted about involving money,
Maybe it's because your sky is already sunny
And anything but sharing just feels funny.

   Here in your world filled with stuff,
   Just about how much of it is enough?
   Precisely the amount that feeds love.

Stop that so you can start doing this.
Doing things in order has its benefits.
What comes next should be what best fits.

Preparation will be behind you soon,
Like the dawn behind the afternoon,
You are emerging from your cocoon.

Are you being deeply heard,
Deeper than the actual words?
Answer this question first.

Though this kind of treatment you detest,
Imagine they're giving you their very best
And when they improve, will give the rest.

Who needs age to be a measure of how reliant?
Let getting older be your license to be defiant
Of anything that requires you to be compliant.

Listen only lightly to those who boast
And claim of anything to know the most.
For now let them serve as humor's host.

Not everybody likes laughter or a smile
From not having shared either in a while
But yours will remind them to reconcile.

Tip your chin up, because you don't know
Who is watching and needs you to show
An example of gracefully making it so.

There is another self inside You
Who would love to be invited to
Show off talents you never knew.

Are you spending enough
Time tilting your chin up
And expressing self-love?

In all of this there is a seed of joy
That to grow will need you to employ
Not a few thoughts, but a whole convoy.

Thank the one who never hid -
The one who'd catch you if you slid,
The one who caught you last time you did.

See for yourself - not through a filter
And immediately spot what's off-kilter
Between what's new and what's familiar.

Everything you do affects something else,
But rather than hiding inside your shell,
Acknowledge this and use everything well.

When you want to, you ignore what's rude.
When you want to, you replace your mood.
When you want to, you pass right through.

Perhaps success was your assumed goal,
But another journey - one of the soul -
Will deepen your definition of whole.

Stop yourself from cleaning their floors.
Stop taking on their overlooked chores -
Their inner dwelling simply isn't yours.

Even in the darkest one of your moods,
Even if there is barely a sliver of moon,
Toward that, all of your attention tune.

There is too much to get done right now
For you to be constantly reinventing how;
Only constant daily execution is allowed.

Allow negativity to exhaust itself out -
To hoot, holler, fuss or scramble about.
True positivity has no message to shout.

Whatever wanted you to feel justified,
Probably doesn't even realize it lied
By dividing the whole up into sides.

Kindness will heal you from within when
You touch wherever your blockage begins.
Illness versus love? The heart will win.

In less time than it takes to blink,
Certain tones trigger your instinct:
Do what you can to objectively think.

You're wonderful, not for what you think
But for what is more You than instinct -
For the way your love keeps you linked.

You're here now to experience surprise,
To experience disbelieving your eyes -
To feel more inexperienced than wise.

Before you march to the beat of their drum,
Do you know where they are coming from?
Would you join all of them, or only some?

Those are just the actual tasks.
Find those who can help, and ask.
Be visionary. Let others be fast.

The value comes from what you don't get.
Endless options remain within "not yet,"
Which means no goal is ever truly unmet.

To you, it feels like a poisonous thing.
To them, the holy ritual of complaining
Is worth their unquestioned sacrificing.

Whether it's accurate, sensible or not,
You should just decide what you've got
And decide to make it add up to a lot.

Sometimes you actually have to ask,
Whether or not you deem it your task
Because others are depending on that.

Waiting can serve as a precious aspect
In pursuing a goal and looking ahead.
Anticipation can be energy well spent.

Treasure those who hear your intention.
Treasure those who pay close attention.
Treasure those who are your reflection.

You do not need to be keeping close track,
But do realize when you're being set back
By the ones who have that uncanny knack.

All of the things for which you yearn -
Put them on the fire and let them burn.
Wealth is who you are before you earn.

You have a pattern when you get tired
And end up doing things that backfire;
If you decide, this can all be rewired.

Pull yourself away from a daily routine
To talk to someone you do not normally,
Who is sure to have just what you need.

"I don't understand why they act so..."
Is an attempt to forget what you know:
That everyone has their own way to grow.

It only seems they took advantage of you,
That is, in fact, very far from the truth:
You freely gave - the thief was the fool.

Say what you enjoy. Tell yourself every day.
For finding your path, this is the best way.
What better road than the one your joy paves!

Now get outside - breathe in some air.
You stagnate in here. Go get out there.
Be out with Nature and without a care.

Wanting it all is a part of being human;
But you will only be truly wealthy when
You let the strings of attachment loosen.

Without any of it, you'll still be you;
Not your oldest things, not what's new,
But what notices points to your truth.

Come out from that fixed point of view
That used very limited concepts of you.
You will become whatever you need to.

How necessary each and every mistake is:
Flawless for triggering learning within.
Bow to lessons that come from each miss.

Keep trying, but not to please anyone.
Keep trying until the sunlight is done.
Keep trying because You are the One.

If it were time to, you'd already know.
It is time to produce, so less is shown.
It is time to recognize your very own.

CHAPTER 16

Dive into a deep moment of thought
To appreciate everything you've got
And be grateful for what you're not.

Become bored by villains, plots and twists
That busy your mind yet all wisdom miss;
Lovingly trust where each one's role fits.

If you leave, you can never go back
To the same place - you lose track;
But new adventures you will attract.

Expectation ruins things' natural appeal
By framing each as a give-and-take deal:
Life's as wonderful as you're able to feel.

No matter how urgent the tasks,
Partnership first, deadlines last;
You should not even have to ask.

Harmony stays silent when one voice sings,
But chimes in the moment that others ring,
So invite the challenge a new sound brings.

Think long-term but act right now.
Long-term thinking shapes your how
And uses your lifetime as its plow.

Who would you be happiest to see again?
Here they are! This is not play pretend,
Rather a bit of your awareness to mend.

The pieces are coming together perfectly
With some imagination you'll clearly see
Not far ahead, the breakthrough opening.

There is nothing you can do
Except what you came here to:
Let that pass right on through.

Time will sweep away all these details.
Your explanations' uses eventually fail.
Take this chance to pull back your veil.

Stretch this past the comfortable limit.
If there's anything more to give, give it.
What you are now tapping into is spirit.

You have an advantage you're not revealing -
That certain habits simply aren't appealing.
Use this as you head into deeper healing.

Deciding to stay here was not wrong.
You'll be glad you didn't go along:
You've learned a new way to respond.

What they took from you is so small.
Don't even bother to make that call.
Figure out what happened, that's all.

Stand by your truth in every situation.
No matter what their latest permutation,
It still goes against your inclination.

Listen to yourself, but not too terribly much.
Sometimes with thinking, enough is enough.
Consciously wait to meet what else comes up.

If you find yourself repeating yourself
Take your common sense off of the shelf
For it's time to listen to someone else.

Allow everyone the same room for mistakes.
Allow everyone room so it is never too late.
Allow everyone room to do something great.

You'll be amazed. Just take another look:
See how much everyone loved it and took?
Remember which spices you used to cook?

When it does not feel worth the price,
Something from beyond your daily life
Is trying to speak to you from inside.

That wasn't forward - it was a wider loop;
Enough reinvention. It's time to execute,
To trust in your process and be resolute.

Whether or not they're even aware,
They're making you the best out there;
Why not take them up on their dare?

There was a time to be more intense,
Now that time is back behind a fence;
Here in the open, follow your sense.

Keep your mission fresh by sitting down,
Not by checking in with everyone around,
But by being here with what you've found.

Step outside and invite others to join in
So that something truly great can begin:
The start of a many-member expedition.

It doesn't matter how long it takes you
Because that which appears to delay you
Only proves it's impossible to sway you.

Be true and truth won't be hard to find.
Be forgiving and everyone will be kind.
Be brave and you will unlock your mind.

Deciding whether to move on to the next
Implies that this you knows what's best;
Come up with a more thorough self-test.

Keep your heart flame burning brightest.
Though others ask you to tend to the rest
Stoke what brings warmth to your chest.

First figure out if they're hearing you
Before starting to figure out what to do,
Or else you will be continuing the loop.

Everyone is unique in a different way so
Forgive and forget with no bit of delay;
Sun, let each of them be to you, a Ray.

All it means is it's not yet your time;
Though you hear otherwise from the mind,
There is more left to peel of your rind.

Be mindful of whatever deal you request,
Because it does not serve your interest
To finagle a way out of a pivotal test.

Again they're asking you to play a game
Which each and every time ends the same:
With you wondering why you ever came.

Hold your humor close to your heart,
To greet with laughter, not tear apart
Anyone bumping into your day's cart.

There are golden people in your history
Reminders that you are more than worthy
Of a loving living and of living lovingly.

Grant someone something unforgettable -
Without any occasion particularly special
Sincerely tell someone they are beautiful.

    Be generous without sparing.
    Be unique without comparing.
    Be hilarious without caring.

Travel in an unplanned direction.
Make a new, unlikely connection.
Express what you rarely mention.

That is the sea, but you are on land;
So you must go where there is sand,
To hold both elements in one hand.

Shrinking from it can only shrink you
So be brave and come out to introduce
    Yourself and offer terms for a truce.

Just because they haven't given truth,
That does not invite you to do so too:
It shows you words are toys or tools.

Part of your work must be shrouded,
Somewhere you alone are allowed in,
So your center does not get crowded.

You get a certain number every day
Of focused decisions you can make;
Don't waste them on what can wait.

Right now your role is to fully support,
Not to investigate, criticize or resort -
Any other approach will only fall short.

Key people will be there along the way,
With just the right word to know to say
To instruct you in how not to overpay.

You may disagree your way was rough,
But their feedback should be enough
To prove you should shed some stuff.

Check in with your heart either way.
It is the only thing on any given day
With adivice on all you think or say.

Find mentors to learn what's not obvious,
Things that can't be seen by the audience:
How the pursuit itself is what's glorious.

Take lightly this present role
And today will simply unfold
Without a complicated goal.

There is something to be said for focus.
It trains us to set up our own locus of
Sharp thought so nothing can yolk us.

Self-sabotage is stealthy and merciless.
So as each new thing invites your best,
Keep a loving eye on what you do next.

Yes, your instinct is perfectly right.
The time has indeed come to fight:
Battle your resistance with insight.

Is your initial intention still here?
Do you honor it or just keep it near?
Could it redefine what you hold dear?

Sometimes those feelings can overwhelm,
But keep heading to the center of yourself:
And you will soon be back in your realm.

One way to look at your workload is this:
Is it something you'd help someone with?
Then you too, deserve some help with it.

History says you should do a bit more
To turn into real this vision of yours;
Feel free to make preparations galore.

Moods run in cycles, but something remains
In you always unmoved - forever unchanged.
Hearing its voice makes the moods run away.

Their advice might sound too abrasive,
Yet be worthwhile once you do face it.
It's given. You decide when it's taken.

Allow them to frown upon your quietude,
To disapprove and demand more of you -
You keep still until you have no mood.

It is good to face occasional doom
To be reminded not later but soon
To keep your adaptability in tune.

Tranquility is something all your own -
Something that lives within your bones,
Something that in your posture shows.

As of this moment, you are on vacation.
You have reached a dreamy destination,
Perfectly prepared by your imagination.

To call one thing bad or another worse
Is like living under a self-spoken curse;
Find out and speak of what is best first.

What feels like a child's shiny new toy
Should not be thought of as a real joy;
Long-lasting bliss is slower to deploy.

Go where there is an active vibration
And leave where you smell stagnation -
That's all you need. Oh, and patience.

Stand guard at the gate of your mouth
And keep what preys upon judgment out
By honoring what being well is about.

The rules you rage about were all fake,
Placed along your path for you to break
And live a life none but you regulates.

There is nothing more you need to hear
From those who ongoingly pull your ear
Because you need concentration to steer.

You have amassed some great friendships
The kind that you know will be endless
Because you laugh yourselves senseless.

As long as you don't get too attached,
You will stay nimble enough to attract
The perfectly timed and placed contact.

What you are feeling is a warming sunrise,
The hope that comes with a new enterprise,
And sheds enough light to help you clarify.

Whenever possible, look to make rituals
Because that which you can make habitual
Is an investment paying daily residuals.

There is nothing that you "have to" do
Except to stay uncompromisingly true
To what stirs up the passion in you.

More important than having a plan
Is being tired of where you stand,
And trusting your own two hands.

In order to set the best possible tone,
Stay focused on what you actually own
And be willing and able to begin alone.

Security will take a different form -
One that cannot be lived in or worn
Yet can keep you every bit as warm.

When we're embarrassed, we deny -
Which is a nearly-convincing lie;
Give honest embarrassment a try.

Don't step outside of it, not just yet
Because the chapter that's coming next
Is guaranteed to become your very best.

Raise it high enough to see the heavens
But keep it where it is still relevant
Both in what's said and in what is meant.

If for a moment you could recognize
Through it all, how easily you glide
You would stop being so surprised.

Fall no farther past where you are safe.
You know the place you should never stay
That can far more than just time waste.

Where is your backup plan based?
What would you do, just in case?
Are these thoughts you ever face?

If you can choose to be kind or be right,
Choose to be One who prefers to be nice
And yields lovingly by remaining light.

There is a life patiently waiting for you,
Waiting for you to live this one truth -
That it is time to entrust others to do.

Move it into the center of your efforts,
Not because it needs to be there forever,
But because you need it more than ever.

It is time to say that this is enough,
That you are ready to call this done,
That you are finally prepared to run.

Instead of considering yourself uneven,
Notice the changing in your reasons:
Appreciate all your internal seasons.

Have you come to understand more about love?
Have you come to accept that you are enough?
Have you come to look inward and not above?

Letting others decide your time's terms
Is letting your field be farmed by worms:
You be the one who rejects or confirms.

Tell it your way, with nothing held back
Because others need your example to pack
For their journeys off the beaten track.

Routine will pull both shoulders in.
You pull right back and you will win;
Likewise, gravity cannot beat a grin.

All of the signs are in front of your face:
This is meant to be a journey, not a race.
So, which thoughts is it time to replace?

Right now, focus on the necessary tasks -
The ones you need to do for when they ask
Whether you possess all you need to have.

Don't get caught up identifying them -
Allies or adversaries, foes or friends,
Since everyone benefits you by the end.

Everything deserves full consideration -
How to respond when in conversation and
When to slip into silent contemplation.

Just done daily, some things dig a grave
Just done daily, some things years save
Just done daily, choosing earns or pays.

As long as you keep believing reasons,
This will take you many more seasons.
Why not decide more delay is treason?

If you say this is the last time,
Do you say it with your mind?
Or are the words of a soul kind?

CHAPTER 17

When thrown off course, orient yourself.
Do an assessment of your overall health.
Keep track daily of what you last felt.

Set a price that is more than monetary,
One that includes attitude and belief;
So with every sale you feel increase.

Make sure your work is wisely invested
Not into what's just casually suggested
But into concepts that are time-tested.

Take lightly the commentary of a critic
Who preferred to look for the fault in it
Rather than stand for, beside or within.

Though you feel broken, you are stronger.
Be brave and let this last a little bit longer.
Impatience is your only enemy to conquer.

You are not your skills, you are more -
The embodiment of what all is in store;
You are an exception, not a therefore.

Try pleasant, flexible and eager today,
And if blocked, creatively another way.
Get your chosen results, come what may.

How you feel when you're at your best
Is exactly what it means to feel blessed,
Or to breathe more from belly than chest.

Let an alternative appeal to you instead.
Let all those rules be broken if not bent.
Let your inner answer be, "It depends."

That story has its own length and limits.
You don't, even if you put yourself in it.
Energy overflows whatever it tries to fit.

Console yourself - it is not about you
But about what they are going through,
Searching their inner world for truth.

To help others to self-attune
Create more than you consume.
If you need time, make room.

You bear as much as you can surmount -
More of a feeling than measurable amount
So gauge by your heart, not a headcount.

Everyone else may say the answer is clear;
Let them go that way - you stay right here.
It is about living in a way that is sincere.

You've reached the end of standing still.
Once you get moving your momentum will
Either learn or lease any required skill.

Don't think much about whether it will,
Just pay attention to honing your skill
And forget even the idea of an 'until.'

You're likely upset over the wrong thing,
Like ignoring music while trying to sing;
Useful anger harmonizes but doesn't cling.

      Rather than impress,
      Take sincerity's test:
      Use gain to own less.

Give your likes and dislikes equal say.
Take no sides until things are underway.
Whichever asks more of you, by it stay.

Blaming yourself for the setting sun, or
Bragging over wars your ancestors won?
Neither serves, so both can be given up.

Sometimes you have to put yourself last -
Because sometimes help has to come fast.
Sometimes you have to bear all the tasks.

Look at what's actually there,
Not the fog that fills the air,
But at what has been prepared.

Be as deaf ears to their negative words.
Mind your manners as you inwardly turn.
Save hearing for what helps to be heard.

Next, get up every single day,
And do it the same exact way,
Until you can knowingly say.

Something unmistakable fills your eyes.
Something about you can shift the tides.
Something in you just makes this right.

If you only do what comes naturally,
You'll only live within probability:
Let others acknowledge difficulty.

That is a place you need to escape.
Get out. Don't return. Do not wait.
Some things are nothing to leave to fate.

Forget what you've been reading -
The kind of day you're completing
Is what decides what to be eating.

Prestige rarely welcomes change, so
Be wary of talk that's full of names.
Keep your words strong and plain.

There is such a gentle wisdom in small talk.
It invites you to take a seemingly short walk
That brings overthinking's march to a halt.

>Invite people, not to change,
>But to find their best range;
>This is how you both gain.

Some things are simply here to refuse -
To remind you you should always choose
Bare feet rather than too-tight shoes.

It does not have to feel good every day
So long as it still makes sense to stay
On a path that heads this general way.

Someone is waiting at your next plateau
With climbing details you need to know:
Which rocks to dodge and which to hold.

The lesson is that when in a game,
If your opponent's remain the same,
You win when your tactics change.

Step outside of it, and walk its edges.
Get to where you can see how precious
It all is - even the tiny imperfections.

If it requires a skilled memory,
Its importance is only temporary.
Instead master what's "ordinary."

When negativity shows up, it's only a guest
With lots of questions, but not with a test;
Work on the helpful ones, ignore the rest.

No one knows what they're talking about
Except for the inner voice with no mouth.
Listen so well you become deaf to all doubt.

Do you think of your schedule like a contract?
You could also treat it somethhing like a map.
Let there be consequences for going off track.

Escape your own rules. Run free. Go far.
Faster, take flight. Find your lucky star!
See? Its shine just reflects who you are.

Listen so closely, not for guidance,
But to find your next great alliance
Or who deserves your full defiance.

After the plan, the feeling will remain -
Because it's about much more than gain:
Growth is in your heart, not your brain.

On the surface it acts like opportunity
But from a distance you'll plainly see
It's a well-wrapped box of busymaking.

You can make this a deeper connection
By embracing each bit of imperfection
And loving the art of paying attention.

And here is all you need to know:
This is your life - not some show.
Slowly is the surest way to grow.

Whatever feeds on fear, you can starve
Through a harder part of who you are,
Giving those termites stone to carve.

Take the day off for today. Look ahead.
Prepare for whatever is coming instead.
Tomorrow only pays whoever invested.

Great joy swells from a greater devotion
As big waves rise up from a bigger ocean.
What is deep underneath your emotions?

What you are looking for can be found
Without even needing to go look around;
More water beneath than above ground.

Today, rather than bothering to analyze,
Just keep on loving what happens inside
And choose the deepening over the rise.

It's not always your reflection you see.
Sometimes you are faced with what's ugly
To learn about how not to create beauty.

One question keeps your daily focus solid:
Are you solving your own actual problems?
This is how you earn priceless knowledge.

It's time you come to understand that
Where you are going is not on a map -
It's a state that no longer looks back.

Getting to where you need to be
Won't show what you want to see,
It tells what your actions mean.

In whom do you confide weekly about it?
Do they listen and occasionally comment?
Or do they bear witness so you'll commit?

Let how you feel be your truest guide,
Work less on What than on your Why
And when mistaken, change your mind.

You need enough distance from problems
In order to measure and then solve them;
Step back, where your insight broadens.

Even though troubles might be unavoidable,
Become so giving that you're unexploitable
And your work will forever feel enjoyable.

Have your gratitude and yet remain open
To all that comes with what was chosen.
Your future with so much more is loaded.

Try another approach and see the results
But whatever your theory, don't give up.
You're farther than you had dreamed of.

Does it feel strange to put yourself first?
Does it feel as if nothing could be worse?
Does it feel better to just stay and hurt?

Are you focused on your main endeavor?
Is it ready for every kind of weather?
Over the seasons is it getting better?

Think less about how it will sound
And more about just getting it out
It is truer to blurt than to expound.

There are all sorts of little mysteries
Things that are tantalizing to believe;
Don't get tangled in retelling's weave.

Your current feeling can be ignored.
Uncertainty can still move forward.
You can be unsure yet still perform.

How much rest do you get by oversleeping?
Or how is tea that spends too long steeping?
If you can give, why even think of keeping?

However many times it takes,
To revisit it this same way,
Be patient enough to stay.

All preferences are misconceptions,
Your mirror's long-past reflections;
Use fresh thought, not recollection.

Bear witness as confusion unfolds.
Be patient hearing what's all told,
Tend toward neither hot nor cold.

Right now it is about being stable
And doing well what you are able;
And keeping the rest off the table.

Whatever you feel as if you have lost,
Reached a bridge it was time to cross.
Thank you for paying the toll's cost.

Tend to the gentle upkeep of your body.
Head swiftly to bed when it is yawning,
And get up when a new day is dawning.

Whenever you let circumstances drive,
You reach twice as far in half the time,
So why do anything but be fully alive?

You need to be completely upfront,
Even to the point of sounding blunt;
You as the hunter, this is your hunt.

If you press too hard, you'll lose feeling
And then it will all become less appealing;
Have a process so thin that it's revealing.

Body's needs first, heart's desire next.
In this order, you'll only feel blessed
Whenever love has for stamina a test.

You don't have to like each one,
Perhaps not even most of them -
But at least you will have begun.

There's always a way to recognize lack -
Just a habit on which to turn your back
By leading your focus to positive facts.

Remind those who matter that they do
And you will expand what is good into
Infinitely more: the power of gratitude.

Prosper by pressing in one new direction
In which fine-tuned powers of perception
Can repurpose your well-learned lessons.

It is only about this one step,
Whether it is a right or a left,
It is this move, not the next.

It hurts the worst yet blooms brightest,
Wherever failure has drained you driest;
Soak in this rain and grow your highest.

Your body tells you it has had enough.
There is little point remaining rough.
A master is flexible - not just tough.

You are wise to make this deeper root,
As winds of change are blowing through
Removing whatever can be pulled loose.

If you intend to keep life at this pace,
The best parts will blur past your face;
Slow down enough to experience grace.

Love in a big way - give what seems small:
Remind everyone you appreciate them all.
Thanks to you, many more will stand tall.

Less fun alone, so find temporary guides
Who invite you to explore places inside
And take a tour of all you have tried.

Unquestioned obstacles are the problem.
As people assume they cannot solve them.
Your own questioning needs to broaden.

Recognize this place you've reached -
Proof you learned by letting life teach
And take you from your familiar niche.

Speak up for yourself and say no,
Because that was not the way to go;
You need to stop moving to grow.

Make a habit of thanking your mistakes
For the hand-drawn pictures they create
Of certain patterns you underestimate.

The part of you that wants to contribute
Keeps arguing against thoughts in you
That prefer to question anything new.

Give yourself permission to move on,
To be freed of being Thought's pawn
And raise the sun of your next dawn.

You can take more time to enjoy this.
Relaxation isn't relaxing in little bits.
Live a life in which far less doing fits.

You are doing what your past wanted to do,
But did you originally, consciously choose?
Today pick a path that is in some way new.

You may not have all the proper support,
But the reason you will never fall short
Is because you are willing to transform.

Which part of it makes you tired?
Then ask your mind to be rewired
To form new ways to be inspired.

Notice the souls you give the most time -
Do they offer goodness of body and mind?
Are they your example of how to be kind?

Obligation should make your skin crawl.
Duty will build around you a high wall.
Instead let your mindset be charitable.

CHAPTER 18

The beauty of where you've gotten to
Is not that it shows what you can do,
But that somehow you already knew.

Exhaustion is evidence all by itself
Proving you sacrificed your health
And shall now try something else.

Just as a boat either sinks or it floats,
If it doesn't meet your needs, it won't:
In short, it may be better to go it alone.

Appreciate and you'll never go hungry;
Once you behold any bit of it as lovely,
Somehow you start feeling just bubbly.

Giving up the old welcomes in the new.
Now to figure out what to give the boot:
It's for the practice, anything will do.

You are a waking aspect of your dreams,
Using what sleep gave you effortlessly,
So enjoy this part with masterful ease.

When they ask you for the story
Be sure to cover every category
As if they were an actual jury.

If your words are missing the hearer,
Perhaps you must make it much clearer
Via means that bring you even nearer.

It's just the words, and nothing else,
So don't invite your high-minded self.
Fewer words generate greater wealth.

On the other side of that behavior
Is what you could deal with later,
Or handle before it gets weightier.

Take your time. There's nothing over there.
Rushing's the only thing of which to beware.
Slow down as if carrying something upstairs.

If you keep talking about it, guess what?
It is exactly what will keep showing up.
Words - for the mind's wheels - dig ruts.

It is time to get your mind clear,
Not by listening to everything here,
But by muting what's between each ear.

There isn't time - at least not much,
So get rid of random things and such
And every hour give yourself a nudge.

Sometimes you must cut a cord to survive,
Or find yourself living, but not fully alive:
Do so, and reach somewhere deeper inside.

They may know more than you do today.
Best to silence inner backtalk and wait
To hear everything they have to say.

Before choosing, review your core values
Before you let one schedule become two;
Give what you are, not what you produce.

Once you've given all you've got
You will arrive at the very spot
Where you can receive a lot.

Turn toward the changes; face into them.
Courage and crisis make a perfect blend.
Each is the one that to the other tends.

Be a keeper of the space. Take your role.
This is about responsibility, not control.
Treat tasks as an expression of your soul.

Overwhelming? Yes. So just ride on top:
Floating amidst it all - unable to drop;
It can't crush you when used as a prop.

As you train to become beyond compare,
Are you honestly able to say, "I failed,"
Knowing each try is as vital as fresh air?

Stay outside of it a few moments longer.
This will make your perspective stronger
And help your imagination do its ponder.

Allowing yourself to become overextended
Builds, leaving your foundation untended;
Only commit when time-leaks are mended.

Once you understand their game,
You can choose whether to remain
Or find a different one to play.

If you haven't done so in a long while,
It's time to put your thoughts on trial
And sentence the useless ones to exile.

There is so much to have gratitude for.
When you begin, there'll be even more.
Thanks opens for you a spiritual door.

There is a whole other way to look at this,
One that rearranges the way everything fits
And puts you in a position to gain from it.

Feel free to listen well to everyone's advice,
But find the only one worth hearing twice -
The one that is as powerful as it is precise.

If it can't work easily, what's the use?
Too complicated and it will just confuse.
You need to review, rethink and then redo.

It is more important to hold your vision
Than it is even to make right decisions -
Because clarity just absorbs collisions.

Once they go, then you'll have the gift,
Not all at once - rather a gradual shift.
You've been chosen because you uplift.

Do you get the importance of being clear?
Is your message simple as well as sincere?
Is it something that you should also hear?

Just as travel doesn't have to mean walking,
Opening doors doesn't have to mean knocking:
Manifesting doesn't have to involve talking.

Being able to sense a disguise
Is part of becoming this wise;
Do you also see what's inside?

Maintaining anything becomes difficult
If you don't know what it's built above
So take down what wasn't built in love.

Your mind's job is to fish for reasons,
To deliver a why, no matter the season.
To refuse to accept any isn't treason.

You do not have to do this forever.
You only have to stop saying never.
You only have to be true, not clever.

Let today be your best self's womb
As well as every stale habit's tomb
By being all about now, not soon.

You need new rituals that support this,
Or you'll toss, turn and even throw fits
As you grow into what your new life is.

As with the year, you have your seasons
And each has its own different reasons
Behind what it would rather be feeling.

With certain things you need an end date
Not to stamp their delivery early or late,
But so you can edge them off your plate.

You need to make time to celebrate
With ones who can truly appreciate
What in this makes you feel great.

Other things may make you feel full,
But take in more of what's original;
The best ingredients are intentional.

Beware of advice that is based upon greed,
That implies there is something you need
To win it all or from something be freed.

Let everyone else choose their side;
Stay in between with arms open wide,
A reach that is both loving and wise.

You can't be expected to master it all.
In some areas, your standards may fall.
Get up until you once again stand tall.

You lose one thing but always gain two:
First, a lesson and then something new.
Need proof? Just think of the past few.

You did, it did not. That is that. It is so.
Thoughts run everywhere yet nowhere go.
Let today's be straightforward and slow.

If you dislike what you are being shown,
It is because everything here is unknown
And you just have to decide on your own.

You can listen regardless of interest,
And hear if a heart is being addressed.
If not, words are just making a mess.

This is just a change in the weather.
This is the time to keep it together.
This is how you chose to get better.

What you give freely always makes more.
It's the magic little spell by which your
Release triggers endless deeper stores.

Consider things that are immense -
Do they work best when most tense?
Relaxing is all that makes sense.

To help you decide, think of it as this:
Any of those you will eventually quit,
But the right one is here as you sit.

Today let the predictable be rejected.
Let advice come from the unexpected.
Let the power of fate again be tested.

They need you to rush. Instead, wait.
You may see more if you just hesitate
Or at least take time to contemplate.

Something in you would love to blurt out
What's on the inside edge of your mouth,
But you know of an even cleverer route.

Then you will be done, just like that.
You will have the wind at your back,
And you will make a natural impact.

Sometimes the stretch is going to last
Far longer than you can bearably grasp
So draw from tales of adventures past.

Keep your mind clear of things,
Of the What each detail brings;
Tie them all to balloon strings.

Your friends are mirrors to well behold,
All of them copies of the self you mold.
What does each of your reflections show?

Though thinking you should is alright,
It may be tempting, but still do not bite;
There is nothing here worth the fight.

Of course "it could have been done better,"
But are rules to be followed to the letter?
It was raining, so you dared to get wetter.

Come to ignore whoever this truth annoys -
That you've done the work to make the choice
To have complete ownership of your own voice.

Clear the space. Empty it out.
Let it sit (don't move about).
Being Here... is being devout.

Put everything out there - up on the wall -
Hold nothing back, let everyone see it all;
Whatever held you back is now very small.

In giving others something to share,
It is what you choose and from where
That helps them to grow more aware.

Place your focus beyond your own self
To things that can make everyone well;
A broader vision is, by itself, health.

Regardless of what needs you the most,
Life is not about some duty you hold -
It is going to have to be about growth.

You belong where more things are happening,
Where ideas and people each come traveling,
Where tomorrow's innovators are practicing.

You need a day off - a day just for you;
There are many ways to see this through,
And each must leave you nothing to do.

How are you doing with your life script?
Have you been keeping up with writing it?
Do you have in the works any plot twists?

You will need neither to blame nor adore
Their endless pursuit of more and more;
Just set your own goal and of it be sure.

This is all to peel away your eggshell,
To shed your before as enough and well
And to convince you a new story to tell.

Now be brave and put your name on it,
Because courage needs to be flaunted
So others see how to be undaunted.

Hold longer and wiser conversations:
You'll need less time for preparation
By using the power of collaboration.

Words become walls that block life's wind.
Beware the ones you choose to live within.
Use ones that serve you well - lose or win.

Is that input helping make things steady?
Words have to match for when you're ready,
Or else they're just theories - just heady.

Bow to the fact that you have triggers,
That you have feelings so much bigger
Than resistance, and so much quicker.

If it can be bought, you won't need it.
If it can be forgotten, let them keep it.
If it quiets you, take a moment to be it.

Sometimes it's not right to compromise.
Some sounds are too loud to harmonize.
This gets easier and easier to recognize.

There will be another chance for rest.
Today is for your record-breaking best
So prepare as though this were a test.

It's good to acknowledge areas of limit.
It shows you are willing to yield within
With flexible grace - a tree in the wind.

Sometimes it's hard to see from up close
But what you have done deserves a toast -
Daring to be more vulnerable than most.

Exactly why would you think such a thought?
It's like some gift you never would've bought.
It's contagious, so heal from what you caught.

How you do today is what matters most.
Be lively, do not haunt it like a ghost.
As guest, see the day as gracious host.

Is the purpose behind their story
To make you feel extraordinary?
Is contentment just too boring?

Just tell all of them to wait,
Just let yourself arrive late,
Just be here and appreciate.

Think of every space you step into as special.
If you enter one in some hurry, stop and settle.
That you bring peace into a room is essential.

Do you consider your schedule your own?
Do you charge for all the time you loan?
Think of moments spent as seeds sown.

The best of things will fit perfectly
And build all around what was already
So you can grow stronger by leveraging.

No one needs lessons to sing with heart;
To do so, training doesn't help you start
To discover your source and stand apart.

Not everyone can relate to you -
And that needs to be alright too:
It will be better with just a few.

Water can run without being pursued.
Wait for the vision to come find you.
Be the riverbed. Let it flow through.

Nothing you think was done so in malice;
Certain people simply have a special talent
For showing you where you're off balance.

Your thinking is becoming too intricate.
Numbers aren't what make it legitimate.
Next time, it needs to be small, intimate.

Let go of all the emotional belongings,
Reminiscences, grudges and old longings
They're too much for you to be hauling.

Experience yourself not just the events.
Lest you find built round you some fence
Edging you outside of your own presence.

Give them all an unforgettable treat:
Remember the names of those you meet
Because this is not a one-way street.

CHAPTER 19

Hold your tongue as you would a feather;
Your ears and words are closely tethered
And turn the world when used together.

Don't do it because you perceive a need,
But do it because of where it could lead:
Do it because it plants one amazing seed.

Look at your hands - the work they've done:
How they've tirelessly served for everyone.
They probably deserve a little bit more fun.

You never know how paths will reconnect,
So focus on now rather than what's next;
Cultivate feelings of love and respect.

Don't wait for an invitation to arise.
This is your opportunity in disguise -
Being first is better than being wise.

Is your position supposed to stay the same
Despite how the conditions have changed?
No, you are to adapt, adjust and rearrange.

If you want this to be your last time,
Learn all you can, empty your mind,
Then see if you call either "mine."

Ones who won't finish fret about the start
But you're going all the way, so take heart
That you will no matter what comes apart.

There will be another time for sleep.
Today you've got big promises to keep
And need many hours to plan this leap.

Be whole first. Become a part afterward.
First you find your own inner wonderful,
Then you help unveiling the same in all.

Whenever you become perplexed,
Whoever comes over to you next,
Whatever in you do they reflect?

Some will make you want to turn away,
But face them and close attention pay
To find a kind thing left you can say.

There are benefits to looking your best
To inhaling all the air into your chest
And inviting the world to be impressed.

Perhaps what you have to do is be there
To convey to someone that you do care
Or that of their struggle you are aware.

Finish. Bring it to some kind of close
So this can join with the larger flow
And help water other things to grow.

As you go on, it might get messy.
Nonetheless, it is a great blessing
To be doing, rather than guessing.

Recognize when you have nothing to say
And see if some words come out anyway.
If so, to your silence more attention pay.

There's a perfection to the next results coming
Even a wild imagination would find stunning.
And you won't even need to try to be cunning.

You underestimate the dangers of staying,
And overestimate the ones still naysaying.
Get out there where creators are playing.

"Have you started?" "Aren't you done?"
If you do answer, you'll please no one -
Let your silence be respectfully blunt.

Improving your process should come first
Because it does more than quench thirst -
It unleashes flow not occasional spurts.

After you've had your mighty brainstorm,
Now comes the time to consciously perform,
To turn hot nor cold, but perfectly warm.

How much of your day must be certain?
Do you have to pull back every curtain?
The unknowns keep all of it working.

Do they deliver, is the question at hand -
Otherwise you are dumping hourglass sand
Into bottomless buckets of promises grand.

Those who enjoy your presence the most,
Love you because you behave like a host
And seem proud enough of them to boast.

Some small circle safeguards your trust
To feed you love until you're stuffed,
So telling them everything is a must.

Spot the thoughts that don't nourish you
The same way as your liver knows to do -
By checking everything coming through.

Listening to their list of excuses
Will put your mind to good use
Discerning weapons from tools.

What you've done the last 1,000 days
Is what decides whether it's too late
Or right on track or a bit of a wait.

Being reliable is pulling you under.
Change is what gives your life color.
For this reason alone, try the other.

Whatever you end up deciding to do
You should conscientously choose -
And this will also shift your mood.

Beauty is about having something to say,
Not necessarily with words or every day,
But an energy that beams like a sun ray.

This is not a time to be the diplomat:
Speak up and tell them not to do that.
Be protective of your heart's habitat.

Leave familiar territory far behind,
The mission in front, your allies beside,
And be in the center - lead from inside.

Remember, and stop forgetting
That it's never about perfecting
But only ever about connecting.

Choose someone to be your muse today.
Someone right nearby or very far away
Who is for you the same as a sun ray.

Your calling is a task you cannot finish
Because it has the opposite of a limit;
What you can do is love it this minute.

As for what you'll leave behind,
Cast that idea out of your mind.
Be inwardly, then outwardly kind.

You need to have a deep discussion
Rather than just diving straight in.
Gather viewpoints not instructions.

Do things that build, bridge or blossom.
Check in with everybody often, being a
Living example of all you taught them.

As many memories as you hold dear,
Keep just as much mind space clear
To hold all there is to take in here.

It is unsettling and yet true -
What's in them is also in you.
You will lead the way through.

You can get caught up giving answers
And lose yourself in a fog of banter.
Silence can act just like a lantern.

Beautiful, lulling spots along your way
May have much to show but little to say
So look more than listen - do not stay.

What feels like the definition of mad -
Pursuing something no one's ever had,
Is how you stay fulfilled and glad.

What you do is not who you are
Just as the shine is not the star
You eclipse what's been thus far.

Seriousness isn't flexible, it's tight.
Sarcasm is a shadow - not the light.
Laugh in love and you'll be alright.

Giving is good, but keep in mind:
You can only share what you find,
So when searching, take your time.

You think you know. You surely do not.
Experience is a trap. Do not get caught.
Leave behind whatever you've brought.

What they offer, examine closely.
Do they also live it, even mostly?
Are they the guest to be hosting?

What noises are sounding around you?
Do any sound anything like the truth?
Aren't you listening straight through?

As soon as you shed that thought,
Whatever you tell to stop will halt
And over obstacles you will vault.

The reason you're being treated this way
Is not to have negative things to replay
But to learn when it is time to disobey.

The most important part to remember
About going or being on an adventure
Is to go deeper, you have to surrender.

On what legs will it all stand?
Do you have an organized plan?
Study as many others as you can.

Center your focus on your intended goal
And you won't need to fight for control;
What must will just slowly, quietly go.

Are you sure this you knows what's best?
Have you eaten properly and gotten rest?
Are all your senses sharpened and fresh?

You will know when you have tried hard,
When effort relieves you of your guard,
And nothing you've ever done is on par.

Do flowers only grow if there's a fence?
Does light shine through what is dense?
What is the point to being this intense?

You do the same thing they do,
Thus it annoys you to the root;
Make peace with the inner fool.

They're not going your way,
So let the things they say
Become part of yesterday.

When someone shares your level of interest,
You can enjoy the feeling of being kindred
While both your spirits are being uplifted.

To get rid of the stress,
Clean your mind's mess
Through genuine rest.

Go ahead and be as specific as you can,
So precise you can feel it in your hand,
So clear you can see each grain of sand.

Keep moving things around until they fit
(Alignment has everything to do with it).
You can stop when you feel peace within.

That was only something you used to do,
Congratulations! You cut yourself loose.
Look ahead. Never dwell. Simply refuse.

Stillness will come if you just continue
To do everything that you are most into,
And be open to finding a favorite venue.

Assuming you prefer your power to last,
See through the mob's tendency to dash
And to your own intention be steadfast.

If "variety is the spice of life,"
Coincidence is delicious delight.
Fill your day's dish with surprise.

Until it is scheduled, it cannot become real
No matter how intensely or certain you feel;
Committing to a date gives your wagon wheels.

The time to slow down is not today.
Today get everyone out of your way.
Weigh each obligation as one delay.

Whatever brings you more exposure
Also brings you that much closer
To the path that is more overt.

Moving forward means not looking back.
You have allies who'll guard your tracks.
So all that is left for you to do is pack.

Holding space means getting tired
Unless you get everything rewired
To only act when you're inspired.

Cultivate the very best of habits.
When you find a good one, grab it.
Success waits for routine to happen.

Don't react to disappointment or sorrow -
Those without energy, seeking to borrow
What you are working on for tomorrow.

Before any of us walks well, we toddle.
(Bumpy paths can still make us hobble.)
On the way to balance, you will wobble.

First figure out what can be gained
By keeping things exactly the same
Versus spearheading massive change.

It's as important to know what you're in
As it is to know when and where to begin
Once you decide doing nothing's the sin.

This time let the first thing end
Before you go start another again:
Learn to be your energy's friend.

If you need more focus than balance,
You'll do well to stick to your talent;
Work where you are best challenged.

Keep leading your mind back from there
Because of what awaits it's not yet aware.
New benefits are to be found elsewhere.

You will learn after going too far
Where you most undeniably are,
And find yourself a guiding star.

The problem is that story has no end.
It just ropes you in again and again.
You're born free but you decide when.

What nourishes you changes all the time.
Have to be listening to hear the rhyme -
The belly's verse followed by the mind's.

How it feels makes all the difference
As your choices make the most sense
When conviction drives your intent.

Dedicate yourself and get right to work
Ignoring anyone who says you can shirk;
Shortcuts turn into self-inflicted hurt.

You have to get to it, without thought.
Thinking can get tangled and distraught
Where doing gathers only what it ought.

Let them find their own way now.
Let them have to worry about how.
Let your focus be on coming out.

Not everything need be quite so obvious.
Over-explaining proves you need to trust
That a knowing flows through each of us.

If fortunate enough to do what you love,
Then blessed enough to uplift everyone,
And wise enough to stop and rest some.

Yes, there will always be more to learn,
And higher levels of this to be earned;
For what does your heart truly yearn?

You're a way of being, you are not a name,
And that way of being, you can also change
In any way at all. Forget yesterday's range.

You won't always use the right words.
Some you choose unintentionally hurt.
Forgive yourself - but apologize first.

Trust that getting it won't do a thing;
You'll end up right back in that ring,
Until love is all you feel happening.

Regarding those you cannot possibly please,
Understand they have an infectious disease:
Build your immunity by thinking of ease.

What you're hearing isn't who they are
Any more than the melody is the guitar;
Are their words and deeds both on par?

Accept apologies with very special care,
Boldly delivered only by those who dare
To forgive their ego's not being aware.

Being authentic and relevant is good,
So long as you recall why you should:
To stand where no one else has stood.

Is there any more you can do?
There is. You know it's true.
Hunt down your next excuse.

CHAPTER 20

It should be no mystery, how it affects
Just look to all those past failed tests;
Keep rejecting it, time and time again.

Choose to have a plan for the day or
Get pushed and pulled every which way.
Priorities will tell you what to say.

Part from those who sell light to the sun
Whose goal is to do a thing then be done;
The gift is to find how to serve everyone.

It is important that you grow a feeling
About whatever you hope to be achieving
To direct and drive your every dealing.

You gain the most through your loss,
So allow the pain to make you pause.
You still have a distance to cross.

The words may sound harsher than what's true
Or they may hide what's being kept from you:
What's both left and right? To continue.

You may not have been seeking this fight
Yet here you are, asserting you're right
Instead of using this to deepen insight.

If the best of it fills you with pleasure,
And the worst of it you rarely measure,
Then it is one of your life's treasures.

A bounty is soon to be bestowed
From all of the seeds you sowed,
Blessings of a garden well-hoed.

Treasure this living wisdom you hold,
And trust that it does not fully unroll
Until you go and face your unknowns.

Stretch your thinking to encompass it all
And raindrops of ideas will start to fall,
Becoming a brainstorm almost by default.

To the thoughts that have yet to let go,
That in years haven't one lesson shown,
Tell they are unwelcome in your home.

The very essence of enjoyment is play,
So if you're getting stuck, don't stay.
Find a lighter, looser, lovelier way.

Feel it in full, but don't spread it around,
The emotion that pulls all that's light down;
Quarantine it - let the rest of you rebound.

Without any plans, it's a messy assortment.
Until you schedule, potential lies dormant.
Once you start, you learn what's important.

Instead of being the main one to bellow,
This may be the perfect time to mellow
And become known for your serene hello.

Serving them can make a fulfilling life,
But keep checking on what lives inside;
Give it the freedom to revisit your why.

As often as you admit you do not know,
You will give answers one place to flow
And prove there is nothing to control.

What was the point of this adventure?
Was it ever to pile up more treasure?
Wasn't it to put the pieces together?

Just as it's useless to blurt out sounds
Before they have words to help them out,
You'll have to wait for it to come down.

To understand, try to breathe like them.
How air moves can tell you what's meant
And can even tell what they'll say next.

Two lines of loved ones flank your arrival,
On one, those who guaranteed your survival,
On the other, those who loved you as rivals.

When you yourself are traveling around
It's harder for you yourself to be found;
What seed grows in unsettled ground?

It is healthier to be disliked
Than to bear even a little spite;
Be genuine, whether rude or polite.

That question you assume to be relevant
Comes from a practice all too prevalent:
That right answers are the ones to get.

Some days you may feel incredibly tired
And some days may feel improperly wired
But keep on going. You are so admired.

Choose a fitting attitude. You're ready.
Focus on your feeling. Don't turn heady.
It will work out, even what seems petty.

Words that are more than an annoyance
That can't be dodged by mere avoidance
Have their antidote, same as any poison.

Next, stop all that inner speaking -
Listen to all that they were feeling.
All that being wise is, is receiving.

Follow those who are on the move.
Notice how they live in a groove.
Put your whole being to full use.

You will save yourself so much trouble
By closing off into an imaginary bubble
With all of history's sages in a huddle.

It is more important to fully finish
Than to become slave to the image
Of the-one-who-responds-quickest.

What if your best habits hold you back?
What if you can travel without a track?
What if you don't even need to pack?

Indeed, timing makes all the difference.
Act too early and instead erect a fence.
Too late and the action makes no sense.

To not get yourself stuck halfway in,
There will be no better way than this -
Take time learning, and then be swift.

You might not be as aware as you believed
Of who you are and of this Self perceived.
You're beyond anything you can conceive.

Come up with an amazing story to tell
So whether or not a given day goes well,
You'll still be coming out of your shell.

Whether it is given or taken blame,
Or fault put on anyone else's name -
Bundle all of it up and set it aflame.

They're all part of your transformation
Regardless of the details or situations
That feel to you like inconsideration.

How long will you force yourself to hear
Words that roam, drift, wander and veer
From what your heart has made so clear?

That other way has never worked for you
It's time for you to be breaking through
The habits that have produced this issue.

You'll find shiny things along the way,
Some will save time, others will waste.
At your mind's yard, do guard the gate.

> Being here is not about work -
> Nor avoiding or relieving hurt:
> It's about giving spiritual birth.

The conversation is not worth your time
Unless it is of that special engaging kind
That makes each one of you look inside.

> Let failure make the ego weaker,
> Turn you into a softer creature -
> Awaken your most selfless seeker.

Hopefully by now you look back and see:
Progress walks closest behind adversity
So ease is exactly what you don't need.

This is how you know it's your calling:
When there is no hesitation or stalling
Or interest in rest, even when yawning.

Though you'll be tempted to react,
Do not interpret that as an attack -
Keep reading people, not contracts.

Partnerships are your best indicator
Of if you're ignoring now for later,
Or if you focus on today as greater.

Pushing forward, you'll get pulled back,
Because there is a gravity that attracts.
Pull harder. Break orbit. That is that.

Make small shifts with intense patience.
Search until you find the ideal occasion
To alter yourself, your finest creation.

You root in the past more than you know,
As proven by that certain way you say no
Whenever you forget 'as above so below.'

You need to refuse what they're offering.
It is not time for you to be broadening.
You need to be deepening and softening.

Give it the time it requires to happen.
Even though your patience it's sapping,
Somehow find a reason to keep laughing.

If you stay focused on one single goal,
You might lose sight of You as a whole.
You are love itself, you are not a role.

You might know more than they do today.
So keep quiet a moment more and refrain
From doing as told or believing hearsay.

Doing a thing to get something back,
Forgets how to live love that attracts:
Get your material priorities on track.

Whether or not you feel as if you know how -
You need to lessen how much time you allow:
Meet every new person with who you are now.

Who thus far has been the strongest force?
Who would you call your greatest source?
Who when you ask always says of course?

You did what fit for then. This is now.
Past is just a When. Focus on your How.
Give all you did before a farewell bow.

Protect your center. Protect your core.
Above its strength there's nothing more
Important for you to be working toward.

Constant hammering on one nail
Will certainly and without fail
Drive it like a train on a rail.

They expect you to help bear their burden,
And even though they may feel so certain,
You are here to be a light and free person.

Words tangle the truth, so please simplify.
Remove any and all that might jeopardize
The plain and clear brevity of being wise.

Even though you may feel devalued,
Let the crowd move on without you:
You have more that you're up to.

So much of what you carry is irrelevant
But you simply do because it's expected;
Why not bring more emptiness instead?

As every drama has a cast of performers,
Every regime has its mass of conformers.
Have you memorized any scripted orders?

Your love is equally strong in all its forms -
The sunny one that keeps everything warm,
Or the one from which creations are born.

Certain incidents need to be forgotten,
Not because they're particularly rotten,
But because they don't help you broaden.

When you hold firm to what matters,
Even though all else be torn to tatters,
Commitment is your rescue ladder.

Once you are sure, then you have to press
On and on and shed all that brings stress
To make this a grand voyage, not a test.

If you're doing it right, days speed up
And fill with things you had dreamed of,
When you keep expressing what you love.

Every day unearths another nugget,
More gold to drop into your bucket
So dig where the ground is rugged.

When you put your hand over your throat,
It symbolizes you have something to choke
Which is important, so take special note.

Being good to yourself shines the light
That signals other ones to burn bright,
So treasure the darkness of your night.

Why are they here now? Who knows!
Your job is to be the one who grows
No matter what the forecast shows.

Lovingly allow what's behind you to be.
There is no need to turn back or to see.
Let it fade. Let every bit of it go free.

The answer you're looking for is this:
You talk when you're just interested.
When you're serious, you schedule it.

You are best fit to negotiate
Because you know how to wait.
Next, prepare to demonstrate.

There is a journey beyond being the best
That leads to a deep and clear happiness
Because it is beyond doing more or less.

It only takes one decision to turn this
Into what can give power to your spirit
No one but you needs to know or hear it.

Sometimes your job is to observe,
Not prevent, intervene, or serve,
But to bear witness and to learn.

Some will tell you not to be so nice,
Which is some short-sighted advice.
Put people first. Don't think twice.

At the time you did what seemed best, but
You've given so much there's nothing left!
For you, self-care is what must come next.

Small gains are better than ones grand:
Proven by an hourglass versus its sand.
Prove this yourself, by your own hand.

You can give so much you sacrifice yourself.
In what way will this remind you to be well?
With what will you buy when you only sell?

> Though you may still pause for tears,
> There simply is no time left for fear -
> Your once far-off dream's nearly here.

> You may find it hardest to obey,
> That which you now call your Way
> Until your heart has had its say.

> So do the right thing at the right time.
> To the trigger let your reaction rhyme,
> And best of all if it can be oh so kind.

All you can improve is your own attitude
So beware of feeling consumed by a mood
Lest you become that one emotion's food.

The only proof of harmony is in the song.
Find your right by recognizing the wrong.
What should you truly not be working on?

> Just keep working and little by little,
> By putting yourself right in the middle,
> You will strengthen what was brittle.

> Your skin is a symbol: your boundaries,
> Where thriving safely ignores disease,
> As important as fresh bark on a tree.

An intention that is this enormous
And so vibrant it's also gorgeous,
Deserves an accompanying chorus.

Know what's really happening. Find out
Because when you know what it's about,
Your light shines through the clouds.

Despite the fact that it may get botched,
Sometimes your job is to sit and watch:
Patience is all that should be topnotch.

The way to have something to give
Is to decide on a great way to live
That cares for the You you're in.

Make the decision. Yes, it's a hard one
Because it undoes what seems already done,
But in fact, you have only just begun.

Study the sources offering you advice:
Do they need you to see them as right?
Is their delivery honest or overly nice?

You can walk away from compromise
If it requires you to close your eyes;
If it does not, it is the way most wise.

CHAPTER 21

Be flexible this time and change your tone
So your words don't cut right to the bone;
For now, let truth be quiet and your own.

When generosity is the way you have chosen,
Nothing - not even your time - can be stolen.
Your giving is the way to be afraid of no one.

Things are headed right where they're going.
You get the privilege to witness life flowing,
And to see firsthand how useless is knowing.

Is it actual or just appeal?
Is it truly something real?
How supported do you feel?

Being spontaneous you outrun resistance,
Gain momentum and surround opposition.
Surprise them all - defy every condition.

Some things just don't align.
It wasn't just the right time.
It just wasn't the right time.

Setting up a boundary is basically a fence,
If anything should touch it, you get tense:
Define yourself and move freely instead.

Energy goes where it finds its match:
What gets caught with what can catch.
What will your unique energy attract?

Asking yourself is a most powerful skill
That takes as much honesty as pure will.
Ask again and again without an "until."

You don't go backwards by doing it again
Though toward the longer way you'll tend
As everything within asks, "Now when?"

If you can practice a patient passion,
There are lessons you cannot imagine
On the way to what you will be having.

When underneath the shade tree of grief,
Set yourself down and get a little sleep.
You will awaken to the light of peace.

Your body knows what you should now do
And will explain using subtle inner clues.
This is the only thing that counts as true.

Your thinking has a storyline it prefers
A familiar place where it always returns
But it is time to show it the universe.

And if they were to do as you requested
What you built would never get tested or
Show you who else is actually invested.

Do all you can before luck arrives
And you'll discover it in disguise
Right here in front of your eyes.

Be owner - not boss.
Study gain - not loss.
Look in - not across.

Do you still need to have a reason?
Can you just be a contented season -
Some days unpleasant, some pleasing?

The best way would be to have your own
So no one could make you feel you owe,
But sometimes you have to need to grow.

Most of what that left behind is useless,
Except the part forcing you to be ruthless
In turning predatory thoughts toothless.

Your morning rituals are critical,
And when you see just how pivotal,
They become your secret miracle.

When you want to just curl up
And admit you have had enough,
Remember your most loving hug.

Be open to all the voices that are speaking
Whether they are the ones you were seeking;
You're rich to be so bountifully receiving.

Going without knowing the way
Is daring to invest, not just save;
It is the very definition of brave.

When you love them, it all becomes easy -
The hardest situations will turn breezy,
And your energy will flow more freely.

Some will let you know they are timid
Not to let you down or make you livid,
But so you can help them be rid of it.

They will keep unloading hurt
Like a full truck dumping dirt,
Until the moment you self-assert.

You heard them say "It's impossible,"
And in response held an inner festival
Already knowing you'd be best of all.

It only seems petty because of your eye
That's trying to focus elsewhere nearby
Instead of upon this answer in disguise.

If your thinking gets stuck on survival
You'll get stuck awaiting life's arrival.
Instead grow a group that feels tribal.

Love each one and have no expectation.
Come what may, find cause for elation.
Your smile has a life-giving vibration.

It's so important to keep making plans.
Whether they take you to distant lands,
Or just take your heart to your hands.

That you should do more is just a concept.
Compelling, yes. But as a point, incorrect.
What should a mirror "do" but reflect?

The best you can do is to give it time,
Not having that impatience of the kind
That expects the fruit without the rind.

Dear Most Beloved in All of Existence,
You are hereby freed of past resistance.
Love's with You until forever infinite.

It is important to know what's underneath
Before any more of your time you bequeath:
Dig until your understanding is complete.

You should stay and see this through
For everything else it's connected to
And just do whatever you have to do.

Surroundings influence all your beliefs.
Surroundings tell your eyes what to see.
Choose your own surroundings carefully.

Look at everything from above:
No one succeeds from just luck,
Nothing long-lasting is rushed.

Who cares if others have failed before?
Such talk takes time you cannot afford,
Because the work itself is your reward.

The way they keep sabotaging your actions -
They are obviously well-timed distractions
You laid for You on the way to satisfaction.

When you take their mood personally,
You miss what you are invited to see -
That everyone's on their own journey.

Above all, it's time for you to reflect,
Await patiently and with all due respect
So when it comes you will deeply connect.

Who here stays busy simply keeping track?
Who here is giving to get something back?
Who does your present personality attract?

It doesn't always look happy - it won't.
But radiate, even when feeling provoked.
This will end up being what you hoped.

Everything is going to take more time
When you interrupt your own deadline;
Make your schedule clear, not implied.

Thoughts have a smell - some truly stink.
But when you journey to emotions' brink,
Forgiveness will freshen up all you think.

No "figuring out" or "working through."
Just pause right here, where within you
Flows power you've barely begun to use.

People are going to keep doing as they choose;
What's up to you is whether you'll win or lose
Based on their goals or on doing what's in you.

    What you are doing is building a base,
      Not for a short stay or a just-in-case,
      But for protecting one critical place.

    Your mind has no clue of what is perfect
      And just uses that as a ruse to deflect
    From how key it is for you to connect.

    There is a reason to craft your own plan
    It is not so you can make more demands,
    But so you can recognize where you stand.

      If you are looking to be in demand,
      There is a one thing to understand:
      Do with your heart, not your hand.

This thing you are choosing not to say
Will end up getting in your future way.
Spend time while you can afford to pay.

Advice that does not treat you as more
Is but an invitation to politely ignore
While you do what you came here for.

Some things cannot be explained in words:
These are the things you'll never unlearn.
To study them, get up when it's your turn.

Though you may still want to astound,
Eventually part of you gets worn down,
A way of saying, "Stop. Turn around."

Be mindful because your thoughts attract
Vibrations that always reverberate back
To key people who are vague or exact.

It's hard to dream once you're awake.
So clean it out, not for its own sake -
But for what doing it later will take.

Of all the things you "have to do,"
Which ones are habits to cut loose?
Which ones lead to something new?

Don't believe you have to have it nailed;
Learn lifetimes from those who've failed
To make a plan by which you'll prevail.

Keep your wants few and your needs pure
To be free from endless hunger for more
See if of this fact they are even sure;

In the faces of those you don't yet know
Is where to catch a glimpse of your soul
As they reflect to you what they behold.

You've told yourself it's part of you,
And so it would be detrimental to lose.
However, not one bit of that is true.

Negativity isn't anything more than help
To nudge you out of that yesterday's self,
Butterfly, asleep in your caterpillar shell.

Does this feel a little bit past your limits?
Continue. You're built from these little bits.
Trust that everything you do somehow fits.

Getting back on track is going to take work,
Daily moving in the direction of what hurts,
Daily putting sure and organized effort first.

This is when you need to be impatient,
To refuse to be stuck in the station, to
Go get yourself reliable transportation.

Today it's about continuing on
Regardless of feeling the pawn;
You are at the verge of a dawn.

You can be doing it right now
Even without yet knowing how
Once you completely allow.

They don't understand what you're becoming
But do understand when you speak of money;
Be mindful of this in all that you're running.

Limits and delays are mostly dreamed up
Because who knows the right schedule of
The plan your destiny makes from above?

Of all of the things that instigate strife,
The most serious ones work from inside,
Wearing your cravings as their disguise.

Busy? Tired? At the end of your limits?
Experiencing life via tasks and minutes?
On your way home or just paying visits?

Building a foundation is thankless
But each and every bit of anguish
Makes you impossible to vanquish.

Be master of two things - yes and no.
Because they make time shrink or grow
Based on what they block or let flow.

You can let go of understanding your why.
Just watch it unroll in its own due time.
You are the first line - it is the rhyme.

You're able to work hard, that's proven.
But it is time for a new level of doing:
One that lets creativity do the moving.

Because everything has its cycle,
This cannot be forced or stifled:
That you understand so is vital.

Some say to speed up - others, to slow down.
Techniques and options will always abound.
Your ideal pace keeps no feet on the ground.

Have they given themselves enough time
To hear your request and properly align?
Decide before things get too intertwined.

Looking like you expect more to happen
Is an expression you can get trapped in:
What's the face of peace versus passion?

And now either choice will be correct
Because you've decided to first reflect
On all you have, versus what you'd get.

Starting requires you stop sitting there;
With no special feats or any oath to swear
It's about beginning regardless of where.

When has worry led to anything amazing?
Yes, fear can ambush when trailblazing,
But what is in the hand you're raising?

Why do this any way but the natural one?
How do you know new ideas hold wisdom?
Answer these, even if you've already begun.

The best skill is knowing where you are
Even if stormy winds blow you very far,
  To be able to spot your guiding star.

When you're rough on yourself they see
And yet seeming silent, silently disagree.
Live your response to their wordless plea.

Forgive yourself for the role you played
In triggering someone's unpleasant ways.
You helped lead them out of their maze.

For now, you should be creating in solitude
To work through every sort of creative mood
Until you discover your own creative groove.

Be up to meet the day head on,
Or work the whole night long -
Do whichever sings your song.

Why try to chart one straight line
To make such a steep uphill climb?
Avoid injury - not passage of time.

This has nothing to do with being compliant:
If you think you know, then why not be quiet?
Either way, you might learn more when silent.

So much more of this mystery would clear
From knowing more about those most near,
But knowing that is not why you are here.

Old habits chose the thoughts you've had.
New thoughts can choose new habits to add,
Which should cut your time there in half.

Sometimes knowing, you use less sense.
A little ignorance is sometimes best.
Give your mind and your mouth a rest.

There will always be some price to pay
Whether you take the easy or hard way;
How much exactly? Only you can say.

You may simply need another reminder
To be neither a seeker nor a finder,
But to be still yet be all the wiser.

It helps to know which you're up against -
Someone who doesn't care or an opponent;
To hear what their words really meant.

Being whole by yourself is impossible -
The world has awaited you most of all -
Both you and your gift are inseparable.

CHAPTER 22

==Do take the time to reach out and touch==
==Those who are not asking for much, just==
==To be felt, a bit of connection as such.==

Make sure it still feels like play.
If not, find a more intriguing way.
Allow your mind to drift and stray.

Stick to your principles. Do not budge.
Be as unmoved by a shove as by a nudge,
For you answer to your own inner judge.

Your very approach forces them to react;
Check what can be perceived as an attack
And get yourself to take a few steps back.

Belief is a perfect substitute for knowing
Since it makes sure interest keeps growing
Until you find your own seeds for sowing.

Say no, give in, and try to say no again.
Was what you felt worth that hesitance?
Was anything unmet by being resistant?

You've been busy collecting experiences
Appreciating them with all your senses;
Now it is time that you just share them.

As the sun begins to set on all you've done,
Will it matter whether or not you ever won?
No, it never has or will. Just enjoy everyone.

Ask until you find what intrigues you most.
Question as if you're the most curious host
Wanting to hear everything you can be told.

Forget about limits - forget about clout,
Forget about all of that word-of-mouth.
Forget about thinking. Be here and now.

Keep clearing the space you feel drawn to
Keep clearing away from it any other use.
Keep clearing the way until it's just true.

If you don't, then no one else will
Share with the same love and skill
(This is not your time to sit still).

The best use of your time is in training
Because it is both a way of maintaining
And a way to reach where you're aiming.

As soon as you let yourself call this hard,
You put more energy into being on guard;
What you cannot enjoy, you can disregard.

Consider it hard and then it has to be.
Don't, and somehow it happens easily.
Think about how you want it to feel.

What provokes you is what improves you,
Just as waves make jagged rocks smooth.
The trick is for you to simply not move.

Keep on refining your questions
To ease or lessen people's tension
Over what they're about to mention.

This didn't yield because you were strong
Nor did it unroll because you worked long;
Like you, it opened by being focused on.

You are the result of all your trials
All these years over all these miles,
So seal with love all your old files.

Reacting is tossing a pebble onto a pond -
Once you do it, your reflection is gone
And the ripples are what become strong.

The long or short way through your desert,
Whichever seems easier tricks your effort;
Whichever way worries you will be better.

Rather than judge where you see a mess,
You should stop and investigate instead
To find what turned neatness on its head.

Be patient until the right people come.
Until then, there is work to be done -
Refining yourself and being your One.

You will need to claim your own space,
So get away from those whose words raid
Your ideas before their base is laid.

Fine, call this your obsession -
But see what else must get done
To give more to your intention.

Be cautious and bold,
Hearing what is told,
Taking your own road.

Now are you ready to let go of the rest?
To redefine what it means to be blessed?
To be what you've given, not possessed?

Have you made a list yet?
That is a dream's best bet
To get you in its mindset.

You're already ready to see on your own.
True clarity you have found and grown.
It perceives, no matter what is shown.

Although no two need be the same,
Your decisions are links in a chain:
Make ones that outlast the strain.

Sometimes it won't work independently.
Sometimes the lesson is to be in need -
To truly know how vulnerability feels.

Sordid histories can be so convincing,
Yet so long ago that you're squinting;
Instead, give your memory a rinsing.

Are you getting yourself roped in again?
Is this another "and then... and then..."?
What you need is the counsel of a friend.

Thinking will lead you deep into a canyon
And once it gets you there, may abandon;
Your gut is a more trustworthy companion.

Whatever you can get this excited about
Is what your focus should center around
So you become one harmonious sound.

Ordeals that brought you here from there
Everyone would agree were far from fair,
Yet without them you would be where?

While looking for a way to approach it,
Stop to consider if you've even noticed
Whether your eyes are actually open.

Only trust advice that is proven by time,
Not green buds from someone's grapevine.
Who has the ripest fruit for your mind?

The brain will overspend its attention.
You should stay focused on the lesson.
Patience is worth more than intention.

Admitting what's wrong can feel worse
Than continuing to bottle up the hurt,
But recovery usually feels bad first.

Along with being more thoughtful,
You need to be patient and softer:
What does your heart want to offer?

This is your cue that it's time to rejoice
Because you have grown into your voice
And so replaced obligation with choice.

Keep building - even in the rain.
Keep building - even through pain.
Keep building - even yet again.

Are you doing this to get something done?
Does what you're up to have an outcome?
Do you know how to do just for fun?

The same ones who keep asking you to wait
Are the ones for whom you never hesitate.
Do you need to rethink how you navigate?

Sitting underneath a cascade of stories
You'll be showered in pains and glories;
Dry off and explore other territories.

It's all about how you interpret -
That decides what all comes next,
So take care of your own mindset.

If you need proof, just look back a year
To see no one single thing got you here
Yet you knew it would one day be clear.

You know the number you need to reach
Before you can be an example or teach.
Until you get there, count on belief.

Some will do anything to save except spend,
Anything with what they have except lend -
But you will get back triple what you send.

No one can tell you the road ahead for you
Because it gets remade based on all you do;
So take advice as inspiration, not as truth.

You can reach this place by intuition
Or smack into it via direct collision;
Either way delivers you to transition.

While working is fine,
Worrying wastes time
(Waiting is sublime).

When your mind wishes to retaliate,
This is the perfect time to negotiate
And ask it to first let you appreciate.

If you think a thought then feel tension,
Slow down at once and pay close attention
To what's trying to avoid being mentioned.

It is not about what they ought to do
In order to help see all this through:
It is about your intention being true.

Whenever big words surround small deeds
It means someone is stuck in their weeds
And needs to first find a place of ease.

Stop everything - rethink your thoughts
To see if an assumption's got you caught.
Do what you dream, not what you ought.

The words you use are the most deciding
Of what you will be feeling and inviting,
So use words you yourself find exciting.

Even though it seems set,
Wait, this is not it yet.
On that you can safely bet.

In case you forget, you are here to love,
Not to collect issues to then rise above.
Kindness is the hand, you are the glove.

Be mindful not to believe in the mind.
You have access to senses of every kind
To be someone who new light can find.

What do you expect is in store?
Do you need there to be more?
Who are you doing all this for?

If it feels like all has come apart,
This is where your new life starts.
Consult with no one but your heart.

The impact of your work is growing now
It's happening - don't worry about how.
Work, improve, work more... and allow.

Don't be the one to fill that space.
Don't rush to answer. Let them wait.
You're to be patient and contemplate.

Remember when it gets tough,
That playfulness can be enough:
Laughter is a form of income.

The power of your efforts is magnified
When you make a bridge from the inside
To whatever in your world is most alive.

You are not here to undertake projects -
You are here because you mirror reflect
All that there is - you're already perfect.

If you agree that things have changed,
Can you also point them out by name?
Have you noticed what's still the same?

More information isn't what's required -
You should rediscover what once inspired
By working until you are honestly tired.

If you expect the passing of time
To almost magically make you wise,
You need to reconsider your why.

You're not interested in going back to
Letting your needs be met impromptu.
This is the reason you do what you do.

Not that it's about going and going
Or just being still and all-knowing:
It is about what's in you unfolding.

Stop rummaging through all that trash,
And sifting other people's campfire ash;
Let today be today and past remain past.

It will all come together perfectly
Like an intricate mesh of circuitry
If you keep moving this fervently.

Whenever you're tempted to put up a fuss
Consider the urge itself to be humorous:
A burping baby ego starting to spit up.

Why not be novel, if you have the choice?
And you always do, because of your voice;
Uniqueness is something you cannot avoid.

Because weather is not always kind,
Build this with the winter in mind:
What can be bound, be sure to bind.

Here is all that has to happen -
You have to have some attraction
To whatever calls you to action.

It is time for you to face it:
You need to get back to basics
And review your social graces.

What can you do right now?
What can you do - and how?
What in you already abounds?

Put your whole trust in that biggest dream
Regardless of how impossible it may seem;
Above all the vision, and then the scheme.

Let others waste time peddling appeal;
Offer people what you know to be real
And they will pay in ways you can feel.

Perhaps you could use a bit more training,
Some help to reach where you are aiming,
Something to give your lion some taming.

It's possible you're being too relaxed
About what you'll need to stay intact.
That said, start keeping better track.

If only you knew how beautiful you are,
Those other voices would sound very far
As you took your place among the stars.

Is it the root of the problem you seek?
Why not instead find where it is weak?
What dam outlasts its own worst leak?

Free from labels of either bad or good,
Gone are all coulds, woulds and shoulds;
Try, whether or not you're understood.

You should start to see some benefit
From working near those you're with,
Otherwise you should start to quit.

Advice that is not worth what you paid
Actually is - for the impression it made.
Continue to listen without being swayed.

When injured, rest, reflect and recover,
Or else one pain will turn into another.
Guarding wellness puts crises asunder.

Each choice takes time and precision, so
Make the decision to not make decisions
Unless they relate to what you envision.

Don't mistake this as your new normal,
It is more like a massive door or portal,
That opens to a very different life order.

With or without any given title,
You are the center of this cycle.
Your heartbeat's rhythm is vital.

Imagine you just finished everything -
Feel all the ease that that would bring:
Change what happens next by imagining.

Take a closer look at what you are doing:
Are you nourished or still just chewing?
Put finishing power into your pursuing.

If ever you hear yourself stiffen,
A habit put you in that position:
Offer all of it up for revision.

If your ears could walk away they would,
But since they cannot, your feet should
Head to those who speak of what is good.

Leave for later the reason it's broken;
For now, just leave the whole thing open
While you find the best place to go in.

CHAPTER 23

And if you feel the need for a change,
That is easy enough for you to arrange;
So much more difficult to just remain.

Look hard at the different distractions
That offer you temporary satisfaction
And don't prepare you for real action.

No matter which of them are demanders,
You are the one who has to set standards,
And then the results will be even grander.

Thinking about what people say
Wastes what remains of the day:
Think as if let out of some cage.

Breathe and release, or hold and collapse.
Throughout the day, carve out more gaps -
Times when your only answer is "Perhaps."

Out loud or not, you've heard it before:
"Why can't you do just a little bit more?"
Answer, "That's not what I'm here for."

If you thought it otherwise, you mistook:
As it was in all that you ever undertook,
Help is everywhere you're open to look.

Move on, because you are well past due
Leaving this place, despite its great view
And despite the lack of a dramatic cue.

Very soon it will be bigger than you
And that is just plain, simple truth
As long as you keep yourself in tune.

Remain right here and see for yourself:
You don't need anything to enjoy health;
Just as you are, you define being well.

When the time to fight comes, be quick.
Swiftness can make you uneasily tricked
And ensure that to your plan they stick.

Stress is your greatest mentor and friend.
Without it, you would always overextend.
It teaches you, before you break, to bend.

It will be wisest to wait the news out
With your heart's hand over your mouth
Until you feel what this is all about.

It is a myth, the search for direction,
At least in the way that others mention.
Do not search for - set your intention.

It is the habit you think least about
That turns your head north or south
And directs which words come out.

It is good to grow different things,
For more than the variety it brings:
The change by itself is nourishing.

What is all this mess? Find your way back
To getting things organized and on track.
Finish the disarray with a surprise attack.

Perhaps you just don't yet understand;
So before a complaint becomes a demand,
First get your point of view to expand.

Today runs on what was possible before.
From here your options increase tenfold
Provided you let the future stay untold.

Add certainty, surprise, meaning, connection,
A sense of impact and a feeling of progression,
And what you have baked is a life of perfection.

Take the road that leads to more roads.
Take the way about which less is known.
Take the journey taking you from home.

Listen more closely than you have been.
So that you can more carefully examine
What they may be trying to have happen.

You need to get so specific and clear
About what you want to be right here,
Because momentum draws everything near.

Make sure your sources are up to date.
Phase out ones that get lost in debate.
Find ones others already demonstrate.

Even good habits end up in stagnation
Without fresh sources for inspiration;
When was your last genuine vacation?

Go over it again, for as long as you must
Being everything and anything but rushed;
More pressing bakes you a better crust.

Regardless of that, this is already enough
Despite your doubting whether it was just;
Empty spaces are for filling up with love.

No need for some breakthrough:
No one blocks your way but you.
Step aside and let love through.

Word has spread - you are being requested
By everyone who had previously objected,
And by new benefactors yet to be invested.

Look deep into the core of what you do,
Right into the very essence of its value.
What could put more of this into view?

    You can say yes, just to find out
    What their offering is all about:
    What is true in what they tout?

Those who speak from a state of alarm
Spread a conversational form of harm;
Refresh the room with wit and charm.

You do not help by sacrificing yourself
Any more than dying helps your health:
Shining brightly lights the way to well.

You became whatever your life required
Just as you now keep yourself inspired:
    By always aiming a little bit higher.

    Though the end is out of sight,
    Do the rest with all your might
    So your foundation is airtight.

Are you seeing how this cycles goes?
Who and what you genuinely know?
How and where your self-love grows?

There is always some room if you adjust
And realize there is nothing you "must,"
And so much more when you bravely trust.

To understand what makes you so strong,
Let go of belongings as you move along:
What's left is what's never been wrong.

History is not for the rummaging.
Future is not for the plundering.
A good life shares the wondering.

Wear attitudes that express your heart.
No need to put on what will fall apart.
Just as you are, you are a work of art.

Dedication can look incredibly boring
Against having countless fans adoring:
Only one gives you the gift of enduring.

Treasure the aging of your lovely being.
Even greater than what's for the seeing:
How you keep birthing deeper meaning.

Change is coming - it always does.
Not to harm you, but just because
You need a deeper lesson in love.

Of methods and systems be hesitant.
Of your heart and soul be reverent.
What your wellness needs is evident.

Share who you are with everyone next.
Even if it feels like it's making a mess.
You're giving a gift, not taking a test.

Congratulations! Welcome to the unknown -
To this place that may make you feel alone,
But that opens you to possibilities untold.

If it irks you - how they keep taking,
Ask that inner voice so busy blaming,
"What's to steal if we're donating?"

Unless it includes generosity,
It's not wealth (it's poverty):
Mindset is your top priority.

Keep chipping away at it, yes, every day.
Chop what must go from what can stay.
Great sculptures wait for you this way.

This is a lesson to learn once - and very well:
Where people must do things for themselves,
They need encouragement, not literal help.

You didn't come here to tell that one story.
Put it in the back of your mind's inventory,
And offer someone else the praise and glory.

Are you leaving space to let things go?
Can you let the empty space in you grow?
Isn't there peace in what you don't know?

They are allowed to hold up their own truth,
They are even allowed to consider you a fool;
But you must continue to choose. So choose.

Keep seeking flow as your way of being.
Always go deeper past what you're seeing
To what is most captivating yet freeing.

Allow your example to be a bit of a mess
So others can relate and not feel stress
As they try to copy what in you is best.

Take advantage of every chance you can
To tell your story where it's in demand.
Wit accomplishes more than the hands.

Within or around you, force won't work,
Neither to influence, to scare, nor to irk;
Your own inner power will simply smirk.

Tiny containers only hold but so much.
Let this be big, bold, brilliant and such:
It needs to be awe-inspiring to the touch.

Focus on what you're feeling, not doing
And with time, skills will keep accruing
And with ease, you will keep improving.

The joy of having a long-term vision
Is that without the approval of anyone
You'll slip into a life-giving rhythm.

Before you decide, remember your norm
And now imagine it got lost in a storm:
What new foundation would you form?

Today whether you feel bored or excited,
Realize the feeling was somehow invited;
You are the host, so say, "How delighted."

    Keep on coming back to yourself
    Regardless of how you once felt:
    This is about your whole health.

The poem of partners doesn't need rhyme,
  All it needs is space between each line.
    A partnership's best part is free time.

Definitions keep in, boundaries keep out.
Don't raise up a fence - build your house
By saying what is welcome inside aloud.

The news might trigger your deepest rage
  A feeling you had put in a thought-cage.
  Face it and rise to a more honest stage.

    Your mind is less inclined to let go
    Than it is to use new things to grow,
    So surprise it with a whole new show.

Above all right now, keep being faithful
Because they are all so quietly grateful
For all you're serving by the plate full.

    Of all of the ways to live your life -
    Identifying, helping, easing strife -
    Forget about fixing. Pursue delight.

Some offer violence in exchange for love,
Whether in word, deed or all of the above;
Without delay, they are to be let go of.

Think, but don't spend too long:
You may just as easily be wrong.
Look where feelings are strong.

Draw closer to those whose presence sparks
Something in the very center of your heart
And the nights will never again be as dark.

Be ever mindful to deflect the chatter
That leaves woven thoughts in tatters.
Get right down to what truly matters.

Don't go back there. The reason is this:
What binds them together was never a fit
For the energy you've been working with.

Be grateful for having made it here,
For being able to lend a genuine ear,
For recognizing those who are sincere.

All of your options are actually vibrations
Each amplifies or silences other creations;
Choose what sounds and feels like flotation.

Right after you reach this next plateau,
See all the new directions you could go,
But to each and every one of them, "No."

While it is not an absolute must
To feel you have immediate trust,
If you feel the opposite, adjust.

There is no need to be combative -
What you are here to do is forgive.
Put down your shield and truly live.

Being good to yourself can mean to stop.
Let all the tasks and appointments drop.
Raise your busy hands and let them flop.

You're not doing this for anyone's reward
Or because it is just what you can afford -
You sail with heart, mind and soul aboard.

You've gotten all this way without it -
Though its lack has sent you into fits.
So you had no need, not one little bit.

What use is another assignment?
Yet one more bit of confinement?
Finishing tasks versus alignment?

Your efforts had a time and a place
That have at this point been replaced
By something you cannot rush: Grace.

You are your best when you do far less;
You are not You when you harbor stress.
You are so attuned when in quiet quest.

No need to glare at what you want to change
But you must craft perfection in your brain
So your subconscious can see where to aim.

Let deeds be forgotten and people forgiven,
As you hold on to this lived kind of wisdom.
Be loving, and patiently make your decision.

The story you tell has to be shorter;
Arrange everything in the proper order
And you will have yet another supporter.

It is going to go exactly how it will,
because nothing goes differently until
You can master the art of being still.

Drink your wisdom from the cleanest cup
Hold your high standard, no matter what
Shrewd judgment is another form of love.

It won't come from speaking your mind -
It will come from being quiet and kind.
Watching is what will help you unwind.

To make your decision, go get some proof:
Before you move in, you inspect the roof.
This is the time to be anything but aloof.

Do you keep wishing you'd already begun,
And then wish you were now already done?
Forget about the distance and just run.

Put one hand on your heart
So the other one can start
Then each can do its part.

The purpose of a price is to share value,
To invite others to participate with you
Offering tribute to the cost of pursuit.

Walk all around what you have for a home -
The inner place you live when you're alone,
Where your mind rents and your heart owns.

Successful your every chosen endeavor,
Provided you prepare for daily weather,
And just as often, expect to do better.

Back then, it could be chaos and confetti.
Now your pace should be slow and steady,
So that even when rushed, you are ready.

Rebuild yourself, brick by sturdy brick,
Habits as cement, to the good ones stick
Aligning as you go, mind each next pick.

Working so hard is indeed shameful.
Doing so much is a form of betrayal:
You got here because you are playful.

CHAPTER 24

Stand in this. Be in every bit of it -
Even parts that you'd rather not admit
And when you do, labels cannot stick.

Kindness is one thing, different from trust:
The first is the way the second is discussed.
The second is a choice - the first is a must.

Be aware, just when you hit your stride
And the conversation leans to your side,
It's your ears that should be open wide.

Need not one more drop of information
To step into a life of your own creation.
Pack up. Set out. Call it all exploration.

Have you put something away for yourself?
If not, you should. You'll always do well
To keep a book of stories you rarely tell.

Keep going - some days will be very easy
And others may make you feel very queasy
But a climb leads to where it is breezy.

Once you admit these are distractions,
You can take more appropriate actions
To discover even deeper satisfaction.

Take a trip - in this moment here now
To a place reachable by one sworn vow:
"Love is the only voice I will allow."

Seek to be visionary whenever you spend
Because more characters await you ahead;
Some will borrow while others will lend.

You will want to be taking care of that now,
Before it gets in the way of tomorrow's how.
Who knows what else being ready will allow!

This image of success that you've drawn,
Is there some example it is based upon?
Or is it the sketch of an unseen dawn?

Be as comfortable saying no as saying yes
Because making decisions is how you bless
Everyone you deal with and reroute excess.

It is you who brought all of this about
Without so much as a scream or a shout;
What if you were to let everything out?

We are each misled by what we recall,
And yet who of us will let go of it all?
You'll be the first to shed and evolve.

Whenever you think what's needed is aim,
That's just the ego casting false blame;
A most perfect life would look the same.

Even if you're only gradually gathering
The things others say are worth having,
You can lose what should be mattering.

You must consciously make time to relax.
Unplug all connection. Forgo more facts.
You gain ground when you just sit down.

Bring the value of all your experience
And bring along all of your confidence
Because you already benefit all of us.

The reason there needs to be a lull
Is not to give you time to grow dull,
But to let you regroup to be invincible.

Health extends from a healthier center.
Tender areas - use tenderness to enter.
So be gentler on yourself, far gentler.

Well, you certainly have yourself a plateful.
And this is because you keep being grateful,
And each day keep becoming more graceful.

Find out what is actually at stake
For those with whom you'd partake.
What does each hope to cultivate?

Insincerity is still an untruth,
So in every word that you choose
Get your inner voice to improve.

Words swoop past with such agility,
But to soar you need predictability,
So surround yourself with stability.

And if you're only doing enough to deliver,
You're becoming a most careless caregiver:
Your energy is like water - care is the river.

Do you laugh from the belly or the chest?
Do you forget about whatever comes next?
Does this lightness make you feel blessed?

When they say things that are spurious,
Allow yourself to become a bit furious.
But of the deeper reason, be so curious.

Without completely knowing
You just have to keep going:
Your map is still unrolling.

Their worries take over their ears
And warp everything they might hear;
Be gentle where they have most fear.

Do thoughts about other possible roads
Put upon you heavier or lighter loads?
That may tell you which to leave alone.

What you consider to be the right thing
May instead be your identity deflecting.
What is your ego still busy protecting?

You got too comfortable - look around:
You blended into your own background.
You are hereby no longer spellbound.

Instead of unwaveringly wanting,
Question to the point of taunting,
Whatever is behind such longing.

Observe the temptation to be demanding
Or onto someone else blame be handing.
Be at peace with not yet understanding.

No need to fully enjoy where you are,
But doing so will take you quite far:
Enough twinkles add up to a star.

You need to create an actual schedule -
To turn it from just something mental
Into transportation to your next level.

Let the outcome go either way.
If it matters, you'll be led astray;
Always benefit, come what may.

There's no one to punish: be understanding.
You shrink your power by being demanding.
Helping with the solution means expanding.

   Acknowledge that it's time to redirect
   Your energy so it can finally reconnect
   Your efforts with your original intent.

No one lies to anyone before themselves.
Whether it is from you or someone else,
Deception points back to a heart unwell.

   What made you think you could accept
   Not what's special but just what's left?
   Don't, that habit will leave you bereft.

In no time, all of this will be behind you.
And then do you know what you will do?
Feel into that right now rather than soon.

Lean times before and after abundant ones
Follow a night-day cycle like stars and sun:
Do you know which light's time has come?

   A lot of people expect you to -
   Should that decide what you do?
   Be as quick to say hello as adieu.

It is by being present that you have seen
The many places to which you have been,
Going everywhere, yet remaining serene.

Be open. Be open. Be open. Be open.
Let those two words rule your focus.
Good if thought, great when spoken.

After the longest stretch take a break
And see what's floating in your wake -
Anything there that you saw too late?

Tricksters will come to spread confusion
And offer you more than a few illusions,
None of which you need to be choosing.

You need to keep things fresh and uncertain.
Every day, pull back some unfamiliar curtain.
It's not about the finding - it's the searching.

You must allow them to deny,
You must even allow the lie,
You must allow their why.

You took loving care of your initial vision
And now it is time to share what was given;
Entrust it to those who adore your mission.

Everything has proof of your potential,
Whether spiritual, physical, or mental.
Anything you think or sense is tenable.

Put your whole entire focus into the start.
Put everything into the very simplest part.
Put everything forth that is in your heart.

Live for today, though not recklessly -
Live in a way that uses time effectively,
But makes time to stop for serendipity.

What if you didn't have to be consistent?
What if rules were actually non-existent?
What if you only cared about this instant?

So move in a way that is proud but not hostile
Since emotions gather up inside your posture;
Move like someone who is only able to prosper.

It's also known as coming around the bend
When you see you haven't reached the end
But even more amazing road ahead instead.

When you step away and then come back,
Push through if you feel out of whack;
Notice what gets you to stay on track.

Going it alone can feel more productive.
That is a misconception most seductive.
Collaborate. Others can be instructive.

Part of you feels it would seem rude
And part yearns to unleash your mood;
Step away from both before you choose.

Some use conversation as a form of attack,
To battle your ear for what it is they lack.
In situations like this, pull listening back.

Time for a transformative connection,
Not just one that upholds convention,
So start by asking a better question.

Everyone else will be able to relate to you
When you tell not what you went through
But what made you decide to start anew.

Give what you can and give it more time
To mature into something one-of-a-kind
Into what invites you beyond your mind.

Until you can move on, keep your spirit
By being mindful of who you let near it.
Among noisy folk will you even hear it?

Sometimes it is most fitting to fight
Rather than flee what prowls your night
It is time to unleash all of your might.

What they can do is what they can do.
It may not be what you need them to.
Make a decision once you have proof.

Who cares if you haven't gotten it yet?
You can go without and still be content:
Live like your needs have all been met.

For the sake of days that turn upside down
Or endlessly spin you around and around,
Take the shortcut straight to safe ground.

Sometimes it's too late to hope for a fix
Once it all gets this thoroughly-mixed -
You need to be deliberate but not quick.

You're en route, no matter how you feel
So why not go on and sweeten the deal by
Choosing a lighter definition of "real?"

Ones like you are a beacon
And people truly need them
Along their way to freedom.

Your body is an extremely obedient servant,
Following your mental example in earnest -
So think good thoughts as if it were urgent.

Think deeper about what is driving you
As you ponder each and every new move;
One step back shows two ways through.

Expand your concept of personal joy
Beyond collections of physical toys
Into what even time cannot destroy.

Don't be too systematic - let it flow.
Just forget about where this might go.
Could any flower forget how to grow?

Untangle from your stories - be set free.
What is behind you is a disproven theory
About who is here now and has yet to be.

Speaking holds an energy that recreates,
Breathing life into all one contemplates
Echoing - ears to mouths - it circulates.

Keep the strategy but change the tactics
Because so far you've only been half in,
Though more of you is ready for action.

Look for some model to base yourself on
But don't hold on to that model too long
Just enough to right where you're wrong.

It's not true, despite all the debate:
They hold opinions they didn't create
So don't judge, just avoid and wait.

Laughter is priceless. Treat it as such.
With fun folks, spend time, and much.
If hurt, it eases the need for a crutch.

Can you allow others to be used
As you just give them the tools?
This is the best path to choose.

How you allow yourself to be addressed
Is more important than can be expressed
Because it decides what you'll hear next.

Traveling gets old and you will get tired,
But this is how you gather wood for fire -
By moving in and out of the forest entire.

Know when you've had exactly enough.
Maintain yourself with focus and love.
Parent your desires; be firm not rough.

They are easily your greatest treasure
Though there is no easy way to measure
How they fill your life with pleasure.

Work with yourself a little bit longer
So you can become a whole lot stronger;
It's almost time to divide and conquer.

It is time to come out from your shell
Where things are ready to go very well
And give you incredible stories to tell.

It's more important to tell a great story
Although not for fortune or fame or glory
But to live forever as your own category.

You first summon your power by deciding.
When you do the work, you're fortifying.
Again and now your power is multiplying.

Here, new habits don't look like much,
And so for now, let faith be your crutch
Until they manifest what you can touch.

Dislike means you still require clarity
And self-forgiveness to accurately see
That everyone makes up your "Me."

Replace what worries with what's light.
Get plenty of sleep and dream at night.
Wake up to goals that grant new sight.

There was a time to reach far and wide;
Now it's time to play close and tight
Not forever, just for a little while.

Check to make sure that is the truth.
If it is not, detour from this route.
If it is, tell other traveling groups.

When you can create as part of a pair,
And offer up your soul completely bare,
You'll channel power found only there.

Before you choose quickly, check once again.
Get someone else's experienced perspective:
Decisions work best when they're well-fed.

Too comfortable doing what you're doing?
Know you only gain ground when improving
Because this requires conscious choosing.

The mindset of training is a crippling one,
That swears something else must be done
Though you already shine like the sun.

CHAPTER 25

It's already here, just line things up
Like using a waterfall to fill a cup -
You'll be getting more than enough.

You're allowed to bite into moods
The same way you can try new foods,
So mind what you feed your attitude.

You need more than walls to make a home
And more than money to live on your own:
You need to love who you are when alone.

Though you may be swimming in tasks,
And to offer help, no one seems to ask;
Realize your abilities are beyond vast.

What was once the hardest part is now done.
Past-You would consider this You a champion,
But soon even greater victories will be won.

Though you feel ready enough to burst,
Before you set out to quench this thirst
Decide which priorities will come first.

If you aren't being heard, then be quiet
Until you determine to once again try it
With whichever words best calm a riot.

Choose that least certain opportunity,
Since it's the only vantage point worthy
Of showing you who you're waiting to be.

What matters - that you have understanding?
Or that you allow, without being demanding?
Are both arms open to what life is handing?

Clues and signs are all around you.
If at first they just confound you,
Use them in a way that grounds you.

The events that can't be undone
Teach you a personalized lesson:
You get to choose what to become.

You get back up. Do you understand?
This is not a request - it is a demand.
Life goes as it goes, not as planned.

Although for you it was unexpected,
What matters most remains protected;
What you needed least, you deflected.

Yes, they may be taking advantage,
But it's nothing you can't manage.
Momentum favors what is slanted.

It makes a great story, but misses the point:
Energetically things were just out of joint.
This is all the truth that you should voice.

A fool tries to fit a week into a day,
To do it all, rushing every which way.
But life's finer things require delay.

Deeply honor the power of each link
To raise the very way that you think
And to ensure what's sediment sinks.

Believe they're doing their very best
Without adding the pressure of a test;
Trust in the flow and get better rest.

All you need is one little suspicion
To get your heart to use its vision,
And your mind to make a decision.

Listen up for words that sit you down
Moments after you meet their sound:
They will be your new high ground.

Avoid saying things you don't truly mean;
Be quiet in the vastness that lives between
What's to be done and where you've been.

Check in with others just to make sure
Your thinking is getting you to a cure
And dodging any bait that might lure.

No need to decide, simply be as you were
And notice when the heart begins to stir
And when all else just becomes a blur.

They talk in circles and you must move on.
Your silence is saying it's time to be gone,
Starting your journey while it's still dawn.

At the place where your shovel gets stuck
Is where others before you had to give up
And where you must decide to get tough.

Are they involved in teaching or in sales?
Do they come to you as either head or tail?
Do they show you your own hammer and nails?

A certain closeness is going to be required
To reach them in the way you have desired:
Do so through presence, not through wires.

Their praise might fill you with pride
And put a bouncier step in your stride,
But You are why your smile is so wide.

Discover more by observing yourselves -
How each reacts when someone delves
Deeper than what each normally tells.

This is a necessary stop along your way
To reorient, assess and some homage pay
To your process, but you must not stay.

When things slow down it's time to stop
To be thankful for that which you got,
And even more so for what you did not.

Asking why is like stirring a pot of soup
Trying to get just one ingredient loose;
Asking what lets the pot serve you food.

There is no place you need to be going,
Nothing critical for you to be knowing.
This is simply what it is to be growing.

    Along with patience have a plan
    That includes everything it can -
    Where to takeoff, fly and land.

Understand it is alright to disappoint,
Because someone always becomes disjoint
When you use your power to self-anoint.

What do you find yourself doing today?
Is this simply a necessary brick to lay?
Could you spend your lifetime this way?

If someone is inviting you to criticize,
Be an example of other ways to describe
What simply is, versus what is desired.

To make the next transition
And get beyond idly wishing,
Simply change your position.

Take your time on things that will last.
Less gets absorbed when you just go fast.
What is mindfully done honors the past.

That was a convenient substitute for action,
But you're in this for more than satisfaction
So operate closest to your oldest passions.

When serendipity speaks, truly listen,
Not to the empty echoes of superstition,
But to the voice guiding your mission.

Keep changing approaches if you want to,
But keep the lesson each one teaches you
To grow your treasure of personal truth.

The only way to figure out what's missing
Is to stop waiting to talk - wait to listen.
Then you'll be equipped for this mission.

Because that one little inconvenience
At the time may have made little sense,
But was a seed and is growing benefits.

You can be disinterested yet discerning,
Serenely detached while deeply learning,
Bearing witness to the endless churning.

You can love them, yet still let them go
Because one of you needs space to grow:
This is perhaps the bravest love to show.

It's just as pointless to chase the dark
As it is to linger in the fully-lit part:
You should be navigating via your heart.

You're getting closer to catching up
To loads and loads and loads of love
From everywhere you could dream of.

Consider their invitation to vent,
As more like a one-way argument.
How else could your time be spent?

Whether or not you feel recognized,
Keep working. You may not realize
The work is changing you inside.

They are offering you clear indicators
Of whether they do things now or later;
Promote yourself to chief investigator.

Whatever you choose to be your intended goal
If it can be new, will soon enough grow old;
Being with feeling springs forth joys untold.

Splitting your time between here and there
Actually puts you in the middle of nowhere.
Do it if you must, but change it if you care.

You neither need them to agree
Nor be pointlessly provoking;
You need them to let you be.

For all of the effort you put into selling -
Into figuring out what's most compelling
Could you let your values do the telling?

You should do it. You really should.
Not because it's for your own good -
But because if Love could, it would.

You have been doing this for so long,
That even the tiny details are strong,
Thanks to what you put your focus on.

What works, works and what doesn't, doesn't.
"Should" and "did" are quite distant cousins.
Your decision won't need much discussion.

You are the source of truth you seek, no
Additional corners around which to peek.
The mind just full of training is weak.

Be with it. No matter how hard it is.
Don't turn away. You dive directly in.
If it hurts, hurt. Hold up your chin.

Fine, consider this your passion
But see that the mundane is done
To fully support your intention.

Stick to your price or give it away,
But avoid being a deal-hunter's prey;
Spot all the traps of words they lay.

Don't just treat it any way you wish,
Or else you may end up its next dish,
Taunting a shark while being a fish.

Once you cease seeing you as your habits,
The easier it gets to feel and then have it:
You can already just reach out and grab it.

Being told that you "should" or "must"
Should push you to the edge of disgust
Where you'll leap and fly via self-trust.

This is the time to just keep going,
Not to speed up or think of slowing,
But to trust without fully knowing.

If it should trigger any reaction,
Let it be your deepest compassion
For whatever caused that to happen.

Figure out what they're looking for,
Then figure out if just a little more
Would get them to shout, "Encore!"

Give real things - not words
Because water quenches thirst
More than asking if it hurts.

This time it isn't the relaxed expedition.
Whoever stops moving on this one stiffens.
Continue to look, leap and always listen.

Be open to meet those who slow life down
And force you to gaze, not glance around;
When they find you, you will feel found.

We all say things we immediately regret,
So channel that feeling inside to instead
Forgive others for all that they have said.

When things go not as you intended,
Ignore the signals from your senses
And go follow where this is headed.

They are telling you all sorts of things
Except for that which tranquility brings:
Confusion squawks while certainty sings.

For all this to work, you'll need to declare
The boundaries within which you'll share
And around which ill-will needs to beware.

Less-perfect versions will show up first
Making you think the right one is worse;
Choose the one that deepens your thirst.

When you're known as the one who stays calm
And the one with whom everyone gets along,
You will draw to you others who are strong.

Insist on loving no matter what happens.
Turn away from "I'll love only when…"
Heart survives even its own time's end.

The day is full of decisions to make,
So creating habits will help automate
Ones that shouldn't be left to fate.

Turn away from reactive mode,
Away from feeling you are owed;
Turn toward where you can grow.

Meeting their deadline is nothing new,
So it's time you were finally through
And started on what appeals to few.

Whatever was given will be taken away.
But what you've lived will always stay
So use it like your personal treasury.

Would you rather help them look away,
Or show them by getting started today?
Paint with any color to get rid of gray.

Those who encourage you to go back
Could put your schedule off track,
But detach from the urge to react.

It is only about what is true for you,
With no one to whom you owe any proof.
You are on a path that is totally new.

There is little use in being a judge
Of that which has no need to budge so
Dismiss your inner court with a nudge.

The one who's asking, "Oh, but what if?"
Would be better off just looking within
To see there is only from here to begin.

You can if you say, can't if you don't,
And things will go on even if you won't;
You will change all to which you devote.

There is a time when complaining must stop,
When the need for more evidence has to drop,
When you take control - from bottom to top.

Spend time on bringing people together;
You are the sun in their day's weather,
The kite to which they love to tether.

Surrender to rest, don't push it around.
Once it overtakes you, give in, lay down.
When it says hush, don't make a sound.

The ones who feel like long lost friends
Are the ones you can trust, tell and send
Or ask to hear you out again and again.

Ask everything you allow into your body,
If it will keep you safe or make you sorry,
And refuse whatever answers, "Probably."

You've been growing all this for years,
Watered it with blood, sweat and tears;
You cannot stop until everyone hears.

If it is a choice that cannot be undone,
Think of other ways to change the outcome.
This is a skill that will keep you young.

Once you are no longer on the attack,
The answers come as soon as you relax
And imagine strong winds at your back.

There's no telling when it will end, so
Regardless of comfort zones or trends,
Adjust, accommodate, stretch and bend.

Most important today is what you'll eat,
More so than where you point your feet
Because it decides what you'll meet.

You do not have to accept what you see.
And may even do better to rely on belief
Until this seed looks more like a tree.

Beware of those who say no all day long.
They do not mean to turn your day wrong,
But you need skill to bring them along.

You are coming into your own.
That is why you feel so alone.
You're nearing your new home.

Be true to your word for its own sake do
Because new worlds unfold for people who
Decide, then proclaim and then execute.

Made in the USA
Middletown, DE
21 April 2019